THE "BACHELOR'S" FAN MAIL

Thank God for "The Bachelor's Guide." I was living off hot dogs and beans before my mom bought me your book.

— Starving University student, Vancouver, B.C.

Since getting "The Bachelor's Guide" my social life has been incredible!!! My reputation for great food has resulted in a long list of phone numbers.

— (Formerly) Lonely, Edmonton, Alberta

Thought I would drop you a line to say thanks!!! I put on the greatest house party and used your ideas from "Inexpensive Party Treats." Boy, did I impress the women.

— "Socialite," Regina, Saskatchewan

My wife gave me "The Bachelor's Guide" before her last business trip . . . it saved my life!!! Thanks.

— (Formerly) Helpless, Toronto, Ontario

My mom gave me "The Bachelor's Guide" before I headed off to College. Little did she know I would end up swiping your list of "Cooking Tools" from her. When she and Dad came to visit, I impressed them both with incredible edibles.

— Thanks from the "Equipped Student," St. John's, Newfoundland

Your cookbook "The Bachelor's Guide" was a life saver. Here I was with the date of the decade and I wanted to do something to impress her on our first date. I picked a recipe from "Quiet Dinners For Two" and when it came to dessert, "Apricot Flambé," everything got heated up!!!

— The "Confirmed Bachelor," Winnipeg, Manitoba

Wow!!! What a difference your cookbook "The Bachelor's Guide" has made to my social life. How right you were saying "the way to a woman's heart is through her stomach."

— A "Social Success," Montreal, Quebec

I thought it was a practical joke when my sister bought me "The Bachelor's Guide," but boy was I wrong. The ideas and recipes helped me "survive" my first year away from home. Thanks!!!

— "Single" but not for long, Fort McMurray, Alberta

NOTES

The Bachelor's Guide

To Ward Off Starvation

by Clarence "Culinary" Culpepper

THE BACHELOR'S GUIDE TO WARD OFF STARVATION
By Clarence "Culinary" Culpepper

Third Printing — November 1991

Copyright 1988 by
Normac Publishing Ltd.
4104 - 149 Street
Edmonton, Alberta
Canada T6H 5L9

Canadian Cataloguing in Publication Data

Culpepper, Clarence "Culinary" (Fred Keating, 1949-)

    The bachelor's guide to ward off starvation

    Includes index.

    ISBN 0-919845-62-2

1. Cookery for one.   2. Cookery — Caricatures
and cartoons.   I. Jones, Yardley, 1930-   II. Title.

TX652.C84 1988   641.5'61   C88-098049-4

Illustrations by
Yardley Jones

Designed, Printed and Produced in Canada by:
Centax Books, a Division of M·C·Graphics Inc.
Publishing Director: Margo Embury
1048 Fleury Street, Regina, Saskatchewan, Canada S4N 4W8
(306) 359-3737   FAX (306) 525-3955

2

TABLE OF CONTENTS

FOREWORD

Ahead of you is all the basic information you need to get started in the kitchen. Basic pots and pans, recipes and wines are listed. I've tossed in a few notes on the various foods and wines because I want you to have a little background on the evening's colorful and creative combinations. (Just in case you prepare them in her presence!)

Remember, interesting or stimulating "small talk" sprinkled casually before, during, or after the meal is a great addition to any menu.

If you are still discussing food near the end of the evening, that's your problem . . . maybe she'll invest in that new restaurant you're planning!

You may not learn how to make jams and jellies and all that other "domestic" stuff with this book but you will cook some of the best basic meals of all time.

The publisher said this is the place to say thanks to all the people who helped pull this collection together, so here goes. . .

THANK YOU TO:

Joan Jarvis, initial and co-writer of the cookbook

Darrin Ames, our resident chef

Louise Huberman, for the female perspective

Yardley Jones, illustrious illustrator

Fred "Don't Count Calories" Keating, resident bon vivant and appetite expert

Judy Schultz, food critic and connisseur, for her advice and counsel

Clarence Shields, promoter extraordinaire, for the "idea," energy and commitment

All of you were really great and I look forward to working with you on our next edition. . .!

But the book is really dedicated to all you bachelors

. . . so go for it!!!

INTRODUCTION
BY CLARENCE "CULINARY" CULPEPPER

It's pretty simple, guys! I'm a bachelor and I like to eat and drink with style. It wasn't always like that. At one time my idea of a good dessert was a glass of water and several antacid tables.

I have always been amazed at the cookbooks on the shelves of my favorite bookstore. Just looking at the pictures of all those exotic foods was enough to make my mouth water . . . but my rendition of those recipes had a tendency to taste more like the printed page than the food pictured on it.

All these cookbooks were written in a language that only a woman could understand! And always written by women! And yet, aren't the best known and most effective chefs in the world men?

And the complications! Hey, I like to cook but I don't have hours to let the chowder chill or the sesame simmer or whatever for these rather exotic dishes.

So why wasn't there a cookbook for guys like me? Quick, easy and basically soul-stirring enough to impress exotic dishes of the opposite sex/gender? (Sorry, I promised my mother my first book wouldn't mention sex!)

I called together some of my friends and asked them what they thought of my idea and BANG!! . . . HERE IT IS!! This is a collection of tested recipes that will guide you (the inexperienced aspiring male chef) through the mysteries of scrambled eggs, clubhouse sandwiches, stuffed tacos and upward and onward to Caesar salad, B.B.Q. steak and Chicken Fried Rice. Also, check out the nifty appendices at the back of the book. Cooking tools and terms, spices and wines and, NOT LEAST, 53 thrifty food tips to help keep your budget on a survival basis.

Once you have mastered the basics, "The Bachelor's Guide" will lead you into exciting entertaining possibilities, everything from intimate dinners for two to Coq au Vin and Fettuccine Alfredo for six to eight of your closest friends. These are also super party ideas, from cheap treats for the guys to exotic party treats for when you want to make a great impression.

Women love a man who can wine and dine them in an intimate setting . . . his place or hers. All things being equal . . . we have been told for years "the way to a man's heart is through his stomach." It's about time to turn the tables . . . or, at least, set them . . . on our own for change.

So, to all you bachelors . . . lots of luck and enjoy the rewards of your culinary exploits!!!

As sincerely as possible,

Clarence "Culinary" Culpepper

Clarence "Culinary" Culpepper

P.S.: Sorry, Ladies, this cookbook is for men only!!! But why not buy a copy for your favorite man so that he can treat you to a culinary adventure.

P.P.S.: Since time is money and could be spent with your honey, I've added the EPT (Estimated Preparation Time) to each recipe.

EGGS-CITING IDEAS

WARNING!! Do not attempt to open eggs with electric or manual can openers, hammers or cookbooks. Inviting them nicely to come out of their shells will probably be equally ineffective. Take the egg in the palm of your left hand, imagine it to be your boss or ex-girlfriend(s), and with the top edge of a butter knife blade thwack it smartly amidships. You get a nice, clean crack and the egg's insides exit easily into your bowl, pan, or left palm (if you hit it too hard).

Some folks favor brown-shelled eggs while others swing for "whities". Most have a preference based on "what my mother always served". Eggs can be kept, refrigerated, for up to nine months but, like garden vegetables, the closer to harvest (or "hen-picked") your meal is . . . the tastier the contents.

EGGS — CITING IDEAS

DARRIN'S PLAIN OMELET

3	eggs	3
4 tsp.	half 'n' half cream	20 mL
dash	salt	dash
dash	pepper	dash
1 tsp.	butter	5 mL
1 tsp.	vegetable oil	5 mL

Smash eggshells and dump eggs (without shells, of course!) into a bowl. Splash in cream and seasonings. Mix together well.

Heat butter and oil in a medium-size frying pan (nonstick is best). When the pan is hot (drop of water sizzles), dump in the egg concoction.

As the egg cooks around the edges of the pan, take a spatula and gently push the outer edge of the cooked egg toward the center of the pan. Tip the pan slightly towards you so that uncooked egg runs back to the edge. Continue until most of the runny egg is cooked.

Leave the frying pan on stove until concoction is lightly browned.

Fold the concoction over in thirds (like you fold up a letter!). Or cheat and buy a folding omelet pan!

Voila! Darrin's Omelet!

Serves: 1-2

EPT: 10 minutes

... AND TEN VARIATIONS

(Prepare the fillings before the omelet!!!)

Asparagus Omelet .... Stuff plain omelet with cooked asparagus tips, before folding. Save a few of the tips and fry them in 1½ tsp. (7 mL) of butter and garnish the top of the omelet with them.

Bacon Omelet .... Dice 3 slices of bacon and fry. Add to omelet before folding over.

Cheese Omelet .... Add grated cheese to omelet before folding.

Denver Omelet .... Chop up green pepper, tomato, green onions and ham slices. Fry these together and then add to omelet before folding.

Farmer-Style Omelet .... Fry together some diced onion and ham slices. Add 1 tbsp. (15 mL) parsley. Before frying, dump this mixture in with the egg concoction. When cooked, serve flat on dinner plate.

Grandma Faye's Omelet .... Butter 2 slices of white bread, dice them and fry. Dump diced bread, together with 1 tbsp. (15 mL) parsley on top of the omelet before folding.

Mexican Omelet................. Slice some mushrooms, a red pepper and a green pepper. Fry them together in some butter with a dash of garlic powder. Dump this mixture in with the egg concoction. Let it cook. Then cut a small hole in the center of the omelet. Stuff with diced tomatoes. Sprinkle with chopped parsley before serving. Serve unfolded.

Mushroom Omelet .... Slice some mushrooms and fry in butter. Add to omelet before folding.

Peasant-Style Omelet .... Boil (or microwave) a potato and dice into small pieces. Chop up 1 onion and 4 slices of bacon. Fry diced potatoes, onion and bacon in butter. Add to omelet before folding over.

Savory Omelet .... Boil (or microwave) a potato until it's tender and dice into small pieces. Before frying, dump diced potato, together with some grated cheese, into the egg concoction. When cooked, serve flat as a pancake on dinner plate.

EGGS BENEDICT FOR ONE

1	English muffin	1
2 tsp.	butter	10 mL
2	ham slices*	2
¼ cup	Hollandaise sauce (packaged mix)	50 mL
2	eggs	2

Split the English muffin in half, butter the inside, and cook, buttered-side down, in a frying pan at medium heat until brown.

Fry the ham slices.

Make ¼ cup (50 mL) of Hollandaise Sauce following directions on the package.

Meanwhile, poach eggs (see Poached Egg recipe, page 14) and place on a clean, dry towel.

Place both halves of the muffin on one plate. Pop a slice of ham and a poached egg on each half of the muffin. Dump Hollandaise Sauce over muffin halves and serve.

*For an exciting alternative, Eggs Oscar, simply substitute shredded crabmeat for the ham and follow the same procedure.

Serves: 1

EPT: 15-20 minutes

BACON AND ONION QUICHE

½ cup	grated Cheddar cheese	125 mL
1 tsp.	flour	5 mL
1	individual pie shell	1
½ cup	sliced onion	125 mL
3	bacon strips, diced	3
2	eggs, beaten	2
½ cup	milk	125 mL
dash	salt	dash
dash	pepper	dash
2 tbsp.	grated Cheddar cheese	30 mL

Heat the oven to 350°F (180°C).

Mix the ½ cup (125 mL) of Cheddar cheese with the flour. Sprinkle this mixture over the bottom of the pie shell. (You can buy the pie shells from the freezer department of your favorite grocery store.)

Sauté the onion and bacon in a frying pan, drain off grease and then spread this mixture over the cheese base in the pie shell.

In another bowl, combine the eggs, milk, salt and pepper. Pour this mixture into the pie shell.

Sprinkle the top of this concoction with the remaining 2 tbsp. (30 mL) of grated cheese and bake in the oven until set, approximately 30 minutes.

(10)

Serves: 1-2

EPT: 40 minutes

BAKED EGGS IN POT-EGG-TOES

2	jumbo potatoes	2
2 tbsp.	butter	30 mL
dash	salt	dash
dash	pepper	dash
¼ cup	grated Cheddar cheese	50 mL
2	small eggs	2
1 tbsp.	grated Parmesan cheese	15 mL
2	green onions, chopped	2

Heat oven to 400°F (200°C). Scrub and dry the potatoes. Poke the potatoes with a fork several times. Wrap the potatoes in aluminum foil. Put them on a baking tray. Bake for 1¼ hours (or microwave, without the foil, for 15 minutes). Remove them from oven and take off the foil.

Increase the oven temperature to 450°F (230°C).

Make a potato boat! Slice each potato in half lengthwise and scoop out the inside of the shell leaving ½" (1.3 cm) thick walls all around.

Mash the potato "insides" in a bowl with the butter and seasonings. Put the grated Cheddar cheese into the potato mish-mash.

Press the mish-mash back into the potato shells, leaving a nest in the center large enough for an egg.

Place the potatoes on the baking tray. Carefully break an egg into each potato. Season with a dash of salt and pepper. Sprinkle the Parmesan cheese on top. Make sure the potatoes cannot roll around so the eggs don't spill overboard! No lifeguard on duty!! A little foil support around the base of each potato can help here!

Return to the oven and bake for 10 minutes, until the eggs are lightly set.

Sprinkle with green onions and serve.

Serves: 1-2

EPT: 90 minutes (without microwave); 30 minutes (with microwave)

EGG BURGER

1	hamburger bun	1
	margarine	
1	egg	1
1	process cheese slice	1
2	sandwich ham slices	2

Spread the hamburger bun with margarine and grill, buttered side down, in a frying pan over medium heat. Remove the bun and fry the egg to your liking.

Place the egg on the bun and top with the cheese slice. Fry the ham.

Place the ham on top of the egg and cheese and close the bun and open your mouth. The rest is up to you!

Serves: 1

EPT: 10 minutes

11

EGG GOULASH

1 cup	drained, chopped, canned tomatoes	250 mL
3 tbsp.	vegetable oil	45 mL
1	onion, sliced	1
⅛	garlic clove, peeled and crushed OR dash garlic salt	⅛
1	green pepper, chopped	1
dash	salt	dash
dash	pepper	dash
dash	Tabasco sauce OR to taste	dash
4	eggs	4

Chop tomatoes into small pieces. Set aside.

Heat oil in frying pan. Chuck in onions and garlic and cook until golden. Dump in peppers and tomatoes. Cook over high heat for 5 minutes, stirring occasionally. Season with salt, pepper and Tabasco sauce.

Reduce heat to simmer and cover for 20 minutes or until concoction is reduced to a purée (see glossary).

Lightly beat eggs in a bowl. Slosh eggs over vegetable purée. Increase heat to medium and cook for another 3 minutes, stirring constantly.

Serve with buttered toast and a green salad.

Serves: 1-2

EPT: 25 minutes

FRIED EGGS

butter
eggs, as many as you like

Melt some butter in a frying pan. Gently break eggshells so that each yolk slips out without breaking. Let the eggs slip into the pan. Cook over low heat until the white of each egg is solidified. Then carefully slip fried eggs onto dinner plate.

EPT: 5 minutes

. . . AND TWO VARIATIONS

Eggs Over Easy . . . . Before egg whites are solidified, flip eggs over (without breaking yolks). Cook until whites are solidified but yolks are still soft. Then flip back and put on plate.

Basted Eggs . . . . Cook as if making Fried Eggs, but use more butter. During cooking, sprinkle 2 tbsp. (30 mL) of water over eggs. Cover with a lid. Remove lid after 30 seconds and serve. Yolk should have a steam-cooked white covering.

EGGS IN A NEST

4	potatoes	4
¼ cup	milk	50 mL
3 tbsp.	butter	45 mL
½ tsp.	nutmeg	2 mL
dash	salt	dash
dash	pepper	dash
4	eggs	4
1 tbsp.	bread crumbs	15 mL
1 tbsp.	grated Parmesan cheese	15 mL

Peel potatoes and dump into a pot of hot water. Bring to a boil and let simmer for 25 minutes or until tender, then drain.

Heat oven to 425°F (220°C).

Mash potatoes and milk together. Dump in 2 tbsp. (30 mL) of butter, the nutmeg, salt and pepper. Pound together until smooth and creamy.

Dump mashed potatoes into a greased casserole dish. Spread evenly, then hollow out 4 'nests' for the eggs.

Carefully break an egg into each of the nests. Sprinkle the mish-mash with breadcrumbs and Parmesan cheese, and sprinkle with the remaining butter.

Bake in the oven for 10 minutes, until eggs are lightly set.

Serves: 1-2

EPT: 45 minutes

13

POACHED EGGS

3 cups	boiling water	750 mL
dash	salt	dash
1 tsp.	vinegar	5 mL
	eggs, as many as required	

Boil water, salt and vinegar in a shallow pan and then turn down to simmer. Gently break eggshells and slip eggs into the water. Cook eggs until the white of each egg is solidified. Remove eggs with a slotted spoon, to drain off water.

EPT: 5 minutes

SCRAMBLED EGGS

2	eggs	2
1 tbsp.	half 'n' half cream	15 mL
dash	pepper	dash
2 tbsp.	butter	30 mL

Mix eggs, cream and pepper together with a fork. Melt butter in frying pan, then add the egg concoction. Cook slowly over moderate heat, stirring constantly with the fork until the mixture is cooked.

Serves: 1

EPT: 15 minutes

SHRIMP EGG FOO YUNG

½ cup	bean sprouts	125 mL
2	green onions, chopped	2
3-4	mushrooms, sliced	3-4
¼ cup	baby shrimp, cooked	50 mL
½ tsp.	soy sauce	2 mL
dash	salt	dash
3	eggs	3
2 tbsp.	vegetable oil	30 mL
½ cup	crisp chow mein noodles	125 mL

Hurl sprouts, onions, mushrooms, shrimp, soy sauce and salt into a bowl. Dump the eggs on top and mix together.

Heat the vegetable oil in frying pan. Pour in the egg mixture and scramble.

Put portions on plates and sprinkle chow mein noodles over the top.

Serves: 1-2

EPT: 5 minutes

Grandma Culpepper's Down on the Farm Test for Egg Freshness:

Place the egg in a glass of lightly salted water. A fresh egg will sink to the bottom.

Air inside the shell increases as eggs age, so an older egg will float in the glass because of the amount of air in the shell. If too many eggs begin to float, speak directly to the chicken. If too many eggs begin to disappear, speak directly to Grandpa Culpepper. If Grandpa Culpepper begins to disappear, he's probably selling those eggs for bingo money again!

15

SANDWICHES FOR ONE

One is not necessarily the loneliest number. Ask the Earl of Sandwich. The practice of inserting a little nourishing something between two slices of bread goes at least all the way back to the Romans. The only thing sadder than having a beautiful large sandwich and no one to share it with is having a beautiful large sandwich you have painstakingly prepared for yourself and having one or more individuals "taking a little bite" until you end up back at the breadbox to begin again. The only thing nicer than creating a beautiful large sandwich and having someone special to share it with is creating that beautiful large sandwich and not having to share it with anyone. Call it "victimless greed".

16

SANDWICHES FOR ONE

BACON, LETTUCE AND TOMATO
(B.L.T.)

4	bacon strips, cooked	4
4	tomato slices	4
	shredded lettuce	
2	bread slices, toasted and buttered	2
	mayonnaise, to taste	

First dump the bacon, then the tomato and, finally, the lettuce on 1 slice of toast. Slap mayonnaise on the second slice of toast then smack that second piece of toast on top of the lettuce. Cut this "porker-in-a-predicament" in half and serve. Is this easy or what??

Serves: 1

EPT: 10 minutes

CORNED BEEF AND SWISS ON RYE

	butter, to taste	
2	rye bread slices	2
	mustard, to taste	
2	Swiss cheese slices	2
1½ oz.	corned beef, thinly sliced and stacked	45 g

Butter the bread and spread your favorite mustard over 1 slice. Slide the Swiss cheese and corned beef between the 2 slices of rye and cut the sandwich into 2 pieces. Are we going too fast for you??

Serves: 1

EPT: 10 minutes

CHICKEN IN A PITA POCKET

½ cup	diced cooked chicken	125 mL
2 tbsp.	diced celery	30 mL
¼ cup	grated Cheddar cheese	50 mL
¼ cup	mayonnaise	50 mL
dash	salt	dash
dash	pepper	dash
1	pita bread	1
	shredded lettuce	

Combine cooked chicken, celery, cheese, mayonnaise, salt and pepper in a mixing bowl.

Cut pita bread in half and open each half to make a pocket.

Arrange lettuce inside pita pocket and stuff with chicken salad.

Serves: 1   *EPT:* 10 minutes

DARRIN'S CLUBHOUSE SANDWICH

3	bread slices, toasted, buttered and spread with mayonnaise	3

First layer...

2	bacon slices, cooked	2
4	tomato slices	4

Second layer...

2 oz.	cooked chicken OR turkey	55 g
	shredded lettuce	
2	slices Cheddar OR process cheese	2

Put first layer on 1 slice of bread and cover with second slice of bread. Now put the second layer on that slice of bread and cover with the remaining slice. Cut sandwich into desired shape. Now go join the neighborhood gang at the clubhouse and talk about girls!

Serves: 1

EPT: 10 minutes

DARRIN'S DELIGHT

1 oz.	cooked turkey	30 g
1 oz.	sliced ham	30 g
4	tomato slices	4
2	lettuce leaves	2
	sliced pickles	
	potato chips	
2	bread slices	2
	butter	
2 tbsp.	mayonnaise	30 mL
	mustard	

Stuff the first 6 ingredients between 2 slices of buttered bread, spread with mayonnaise and prepared mustard, and ATTACK!!!

Serves: 1

EPT: 10 minutes

19

DELI-STYLE PITA POCKETS

1	pita pocket	1
	hot prepared mustard, to taste	
¾ cup	chopped ham OR corned beef	175 mL
1	tomato, sliced	1
½ cup	shredded lettuce	125 mL
½ cup	grated Cheddar cheese	125 mL
	salt and pepper, to taste	
	dill pickles	

Cut the pita round in half. Spread hot mustard inside both pockets.

In a bowl combine meat, tomato slices, lettuce and cheese. Season to taste with salt and pepper.

Stuff each pocket with this meat mixture, flip a few dill pickles on the side and dream of great delicatessens of the past.

Serves: 1

EPT: 10 minutes

DENVER SANDWICH
Open or Closed

1 tbsp.	vegetable oil	15 mL
2	eggs, beaten	2
1 tbsp.	finely chopped tomatoes	15 mL
1 tbsp.	chopped green onion	15 mL
1 tbsp.	chopped ham	15 mL
	salt and pepper, to taste	
2	bread slices, toasted	2

Put oil in a frying pan and heat it at medium-high. Throw eggs, tomato, green onions and ham together in a bowl and mix well. Season with salt and pepper. Now dump the concoction into the frying pan. Cook on 1 side until lightly set, then flip over and cook for another 1-2 minutes. Remove from heat and set aside.

For the Open Denver:

Cut the toast diagonally. Place on a plate, each slice overlapping the other. Lay that old egg concoction right on top of the toast.

For the Closed Denver:

Slide that slender egg concoction between the slices of bread. Cut that sandwich in half and dream of the Rockies.

Serves: 1

EPT: 15 minutes

EGG SALAD SANDWICH

2	eggs, hard-boiled* and diced	2
¼ cup	shredded lettuce	50 mL
1	green onion, diced	1
½ tsp.	relish	2 mL
2 tbsp.	mayonnaise	30 mL
	salt and pepper, to taste	
2	bread slices, buttered	2
	dill pickles	
	potato chips	

Heap eggs, lettuce, green onion, relish, mayonnaise, salt and pepper into a bowl and mash them all together.

Plop this egg salad on top of 1 slice of bread, cover with the second slice. Cut the sandwich in half, put a napkin in your lap and enjoy!!

Serve with dill pickles and potato chips and try not to let the chicken see how much you are enjoying yourself!

Serves: 1

EPT: 10 minutes

* To hard boil an egg, place egg(s) in enough cold water to cover. Bring water to a boil, then lower heat to a simmer. Simmer 10-15 minutes for hard-boiled, 4 minutes for medium, 2-3 minutes for soft-boiled. Put hard-boiled eggs in cold water immediately to stop cooking and prevent discoloration. Timings are for room-temperature eggs.

EL CUBANO SANDWICH

2	thin slices roast beef	2
3	thin slices ham	3
1	lettuce leaf	1
1	tomato, sliced	1
2	Swiss cheese slices	2
1	French bread slice, buttered	1

Dump the first 5 ingredients, in order listed above, onto the slice of French bread.

Throw the sandwich onto a cookie sheet and slide her* into the oven, under the broiler at medium. Cook until the cheese has melted.

Serves: 1

EPT: 10 minutes

*All beautifully built ships, baseball bats, hurricanes and sandwiches are referred to with the utmost respect and affection as "she" or "her". — Poppa Jack Culpepper's Committee for Courtesy to Womenfolk and Other Naturally Superior Creatures.

21

FISH POCKETS

3	frozen fish sticks OR battered fish	3
1	pita bread pocket	1
	tartar sauce OR mayonnaise, to taste	
	cucumber, sliced	
	lettuce, shredded	
	white onion, diced	
	tomato, sliced	
	Cheddar cheese, grated	

Cook fish sticks or battered fish according to package directions.

Cut the top off the pita, making a pocket, and heavily spread the inside with either tartar sauce or mayo.

Stuff in the cooked fish sticks or battered fish and any amount or combination of the remaining ingredients.

Serves: 1

EPT: 20 minutes

HAM SALAD SANDWICH

¼ cup	finely diced ham	50 mL
¼ cup	shredded lettuce	50 mL
1 tbsp.	finely diced celery	15 mL
1 tbsp.	finely diced green onion	15 mL
2 tbsp.	mayonnaise	30 mL
	butter, to taste	
2	bread slices	2

Fling and mix ham, some of the shredded lettuce, celery, green onion and mayonnaise together. Butter the bread.

Dump ham salad on 1 slice of bread. Top with the remaining lettuce, toss second slice of bread on top and cut as desired.

Serves: 1

EPT: 10 minutes

22

MONTE CRISTO SANDWICH

1 tbsp.	vegetable oil	15 mL
2	Swiss cheese slices	2
2	thin slices of ham	2
2	French bread slices	2
1	egg, beaten	1

Put oil in frying pan and heat the pan over medium heat. Plop cheese and ham on 1 slice of bread. Cover with second slice of bread. Dunk the sandwich into the beaten egg.

Fry on medium heat until both sides are golden brown.

Serves: 1

EPT: 15 minutes

REUBEN* SANDWICH

2	rye bread slices, buttered	2
2	Swiss cheese slices	2
3-4	thin slices corned beef	3-4
	sauerkraut, well-drained, to taste	

Heave rye bread, buttered side down, into a frying pan and put it over a burner at medium heat. Dump cheese on top of bread.

In space left between the bread slices in the frying pan, plop the corned beef and sauerkraut so it can heat up.

Then, toss the sauerkraut on top of the Swiss cheese and pile on the corned beef. Close that sandwich and cut into desired (and desirable) sizes.

Serve with garnish of your choice.

Serves: 1

EPT: 15 minutes

*The Culpepper clan salutes Reuben (whoever he was?) for having such a lovely sandwich named after him with this brief ode by one of our least offensive "Oders", Charichi Culpepper.

> **Reuben, Reuben, who could doubt**
> **Ein sandvich mit das sauerkraut?**
> **Und mit das cheese so nice und sviss**
> **Such sandvich dat, she could not miss!**
> **Pile das corned beef on der rye**
> **Uud kiss your hunger-pains good-bye!!!**

23

TRIPLE GRILLED HAM AND CHEESE

3	bread slices, buttered	3
4	Cheddar OR process cheese slices	4
4	ham slices, stacked in 2 sections	4

Dump the bread (buttered side down) in a large frying pan over medium heat. Chuck 2 slices of cheese on 2 of the slices of bread. Then top the cheese with 2 slices of ham. When sandwich bread is golden brown and cheese is melted, throw the empty piece of bread on top of 1 of the other 2 and flop the third (loaded) slice of bread on top.

Cut in half and serve with dill pickles on the side.

Serves: 1

EPT: 10 minutes

TUNA (OR SALMON) SALAD SANDWICH

½	can tuna OR salmon, (6.5 oz. [184 g]), drained	½
	shredded lettuce	
2 tbsp.	finely diced celery	30 mL
2 tbsp.	finely diced green onion	30 mL
2 tbsp.	mayonnaise	30 mL
	salt and pepper, to taste	
1 drop	lemon juice	1 drop
2	bread slices, buttered	2

Combine all ingredients, except for the bread, in a mixing bowl.

Dump and spread this marine masterpiece between the two slices of buttered bread.

Cut the sandwich in half, think again of a career at sea, and serve.

Serves: 1

EPT: 10 minutes

Uncle Yardley Culpepper got "finely diced" once in Las Vegas. It happened in one of those "street corner casinos." He's still on that street corner . . . selling pencils.

24

THE OLD HOTEL HOTPLATE TRICK

Ever stay in one of those upper class hostelries where the room service (if there is any!) shuts down about 9:30 . . . just as you are about to order your late evening snack?? Hike down the block to the nearest convenience store and pick up. . .

1 loaf of bread
1 packet of margarine
1 packet of cheese
1 roll of aluminum foil

Spread 2 slices of bread with margarine. Put slices of cheese between the unbuttered sides of the bread. Wrap the sandwich in foil.

Turn the electric iron (available from housekeeping) on to medium-hot setting (cotton). Prop the iron upside down between the phone books or your shoes. Place the foil package on the sole plate of the iron. In 5 minutes turn the package over.

If a browner color is desired...place the package back on the iron.

Submarine sandwiches can be made by using mozzarella cheese instead of Cheddar and adding pieces of meat, pickles and mustard.

Serves: 1

EPT: 10 minutes

The Great Sandwich Building Contest:

Ms. Greanne Jeen Culpepper once said "marriage is the process whereby love ripens into vengeance" . . . like some sandwich building contests we have attended. Start with 12 or 13 (for luck) ingredients on a counter. Each contestant attempts to build the most creative, appealing and tasty tower of temptation from the same group of goodies. Put a time limit on the session and have the results tasted by an impartial referee . . . if there is such a thing!

Your own imagination and gravity are the only restrictions to creating thousands of new and different sandwiches.

RABBIT FOOD

Who would have thought that the first leaves, herbs and roots our prehistoric ancestors munched on would still be the best way to begin or complement a meal?

There are salads for all occasions. You can build a creative and disgustingly healthy concoction around many vegetables and fruits. Begin with the basic beauties listed in this chapter and then branch out on your own.

RABBIT FOOD (SALADS)

BASIC TOSSED SALAD

1	head lettuce (romaine, green leaf OR endive)	1
2	radishes, sliced	2
1	carrot, thinly sliced	1
½	cucumber, thinly sliced	½
2	green onions, diced	2
2	celery stalks, diced	2
	salad dressing, of your choice	

Tear up the lettuce. Throw it, the radishes, carrots, cucumber, green onions and celery into a big bowl. Dump your favorite salad dressing on top.

Move those little veggies around the bowl for a couple of laps, somersaults (not to be confused with Epsom Salts!) and . . . VOILA!

Serves: 1-2

EPT: 10 minutes

Colleen Patricia Culpepper's Sure-Fire Safe Way to Clean Lettuce: "Remove leaves from the lettuce. Swish them around in a bowl or sink full of cold water. Take the leaves from the water and shake (GENTLY!) free of water."

HOW <u>NOT</u> TO TOSS A SALAD

POOR MAN'S CAESAR SALAD

1	head romaine lettuce	1
¼ cup	croutons	50 mL
2 tbsp.	grated Parmesan cheese	30 mL
1 tbsp.	bacon bits	15 mL
⅓ cup	Caesar Salad Dressing (from any grocery store)	75 mL

Wash and rip lettuce into bite-size pieces. Fling all ingredients into a salad bowl and toss about. All hail Caesar!!

Serves: 1-2

EPT: 10 minutes

SPINACH SALAD JOSEN

½ lb.	fresh spinach	250 g
2 tbsp.	bacon bits	30 mL
1	hard-boiled egg, sliced	1
2 tbsp.	croutons	30 mL
2 tbsp.	Cream Garlic Dressing	30 mL
1	orange, peeled and sectioned	1
2 tbsp.	walnuts	30 mL

Toss the spinach into a salad bowl. Dump the bacon bits, egg slices and croutons on top of the spinach.

Dribble dressing over and garnish with orange sections and walnuts.

Serves: 1-2

EPT: 10 minutes

WALDORF SALAD

2	apples, diced	2
¼ cup	finely diced celery	50 mL
2 tbsp.	mayonnaise	30 mL
½ cup	whipping cream, whipped	125 mL
2 tbsp.	chopped walnuts	30 mL

Soak diced apples for 5 minutes in 1 cup (250 mL) of water and 2 tbsp. (30 mL) of lemon juice. This keeps the apples from browning.

Drain the apples. Chuck the apples, celery, mayonnaise and whipped cream together in a bowl. Mix 'em up a bit. Garnish with walnuts.

Serves: 1-2

EPT: 15 minutes

Clarence Culpepper's Words of Wisdom on Grazing in a Salad Patch: "A cool, appetizing approach to the beginning, middle or end of a meal, the salad can be a visual as well as vitamin delight."

Aunt Jo-Jo Culpepper's Assessment of Clarence's Salad Days: "If that boy cooked as well as he talked about it, he'd be a world renowned chef at the Waldorf ... 'stead of a big, round drugstore cowboy down at the Griffin Boys' cafe. Still ... he loves his feed!"

COLESLAW

⅔	small head cabbage, grated OR thinly sliced	⅔
1	carrot, grated	1
2	green onions, diced	2
	salt and pepper, to taste	
3 tbsp.	coleslaw dressing (from any grocery store)	45 mL

Heap ingredients together, mix them up good, then serve.

Serves: 1-2

EPT: 10 minutes

MIXED VEGETABLE SALAD

⅔ cup	cauliflower florets	150 mL
⅔ cup	broccoli florets	150 mL
1	carrot, diced	1
1	celery stalk, diced	1
1	onion, diced	1
1	tomato, cut in wedges	1
dash	oregano	dash
⅓ cup	Vinaigrette Dressing	75 mL
	salt and pepper, to taste	
	garlic powder, to taste	

Dump all ingredients into a salad bowl. (Any other diced vegetables of your choosing, or that you might have left over in your refrigerator, can be added.) Mix and season with salt, pepper and garlic. Marinating this entire salad for a little while (1-24 hours) enriches the flavor.

Mix again just before serving.

Serves: 1-2

EPT: 20 minutes

J. J. Culpepper's inside tips: Vinaigrette is just a fancy way of referring to oil and vinegar-based dressings. You can get it at the grocery store ... but use the high-falutin' name to impress her with your vast culinary vocabulary.

"CHEF AMES" SALAD

1	head lettuce	1
¼ cup	cooked chicken in thin strips	50 mL
¼ cup	ham in thin strips	50 mL
¼ cup	roast beef in thin strips	50 mL
	Italian Vinaigrette Dressing (from your grocery store)	
2 tbsp.	grated Cheddar cheese	30 mL
2 tbsp.	grated Swiss cheese	30 mL
1	tomato, cut in wedges	1
1	hard-boiled egg, sliced	1
½	cucumber, peeled and sliced	½

Break lettuce into bite-size pieces. Dump lettuce into a salad bowl. Moisten lightly with vinaigrette dressing. Garnish with chicken, ham, roast beef, grated cheese, tomato wedges, sliced egg and cucumber slices.

Serves: 1-2

EPT: 10 minutes

31

POTATO SALAD

½ lb.	potatoes, cooked tender and diced	250 g
2	hard-boiled eggs, diced	2
1	green onion, diced	1
1	celery stalk, diced	1
⅓ cup	mayonnaise	75 mL
	salt and pepper, to taste	
½ tsp.	prepared mustard	2 mL

Slap ingredients together, mixing them up well. Chill for 30 minutes in the refrigerator before serving.

Serves: 2

EPT: 30 minutes

HOT POTATO SALAD

3	bacon slices	3
2	large potatoes, peeled and thinly sliced	2
1	green onion, chopped	1
dash	pepper	dash
⅓ cup	chicken broth	75 mL
1 tbsp.	vinegar	15 mL
1 cup	green beans, canned OR frozen, well drained	250 mL

In a frying pan, cook the bacon until crisp. Crumble it and set it aside.

Fry the potato slices in the bacon fat for 2 minutes. Stir in the onion, pepper and chicken broth.

Simmer, covered, for 5 minutes and then simmer on medium, uncovered, until potatoes are tender...but not mushy.

Stir in the vinegar, beans and bacon. Heat thoroughly and serve immediately.

Serves: 1-2

EPT: 20 minutes

CRAB-STUFFED AVOCADO
(with brandy dressing)

1	avocado, halved	1
4.5 oz.	can crab meat, drained	127 g
4 tbsp.	mayonnaise	60 mL
½ tbsp.	ketchup	7 mL
½ tbsp.	brandy	7 mL

Remove the stone from the avocado. Moisten and mix crab meat with 1 tbsp. (15 mL) mayonnaise and stuff it in the avocado halves.

Make dressing by mixing 3 tbsp. (45 mL) mayonnaise with the ketchup and brandy. Spoon dressing on top of crab meat.

Serves: 1-2

EPT: 5 minutes

CELERY SALMON SALAD

½	head lettuce, shredded	½
7.5 oz.	can salmon, drained	213 g
4	celery stalks, diced	4
1	green onion, sliced	1
	salt and pepper, to taste	
	Thousand Island Dressing, to taste	

Cover 2 salad plates with lettuce. Toss remaining ingredients, except dressing, together in a bowl and then dump it on the lettuce (tastefully, of course).

Serve with Thousand Island Dressing on the side.

Serves: 2

EPT: 10 minutes

33

MACARONI SALAD WITH HAM

⅓ cup	uncooked macaroni	75 mL
⅓ cup	diced ham	75 mL
2 tbsp.	diced celery	30 mL
1 tbsp.	diced green pepper	15 mL
1 tbsp.	diced pimiento	15 mL
1	green onion, diced	1
¼ cup	mayonnaise	50 mL
dash	salt	dash
dash	pepper	dash
½ cup	diced Cheddar cheese	125 mL

Cook macaroni according to instructions on package. Drain well and throw it into the refrigerator to chill.

When chilled, mix the macaroni with the remaining ingredients. Refrigerate for 30 minutes before serving.

Serves: 1-2

EPT: 20 minutes

FRUIT SALAD

2 cups	sliced fresh fruit, made up of. . .	500 mL
	watermelon	
	apples	
	oranges	
	grapefruit	
	grapes	
	strawberries	
	peaches	
	pears	
	pineapple	

Use any combination of fruit that happens to be in season.

Peel the fruit with inedible skins and then chop all the fruit into bite-size pieces. Dump them all in a dish and chill. Serve with side dish of ice cream or cottage cheese (or you can plop the fruit on top of the ice cream or vice-versa!). If fresh fruits are not available, you can substitute canned fruit (and don't blame us if you get a real warm good-night handshake from your date).

Serves: 1-2

EPT: 15 minutes

MARSHMALLOW FRUIT DELIGHT

2 cups	diced fresh fruit OR canned fruit salad, drained	450 mL
⅓ cup	sour cream	75 mL
½ cup	miniature marshmallows	125 mL
⅛ cup	shredded coconut	25 mL

Plop and stir fruit, sour cream, coconut and marshmallows together in a bowl.

Chill at least 30 minutes before serving*.

Serves: 1-2

EPT: 10 minutes

*Aunt Jeanne Marguerite Culpepper's Helpful Hints: This salad can even be made the previous evening and chilled overnight . . . if you are the kind of guy who plans ahead!!

PINEAPPLE SALAD DELIGHT

1	pineapple, halved	1
2 tsp.	sugar	10 mL
1 tsp.	Grand Marnier	5 mL
2	scoops vanilla ice cream	2

Cut a ripe pineapple in half lengthwise. Carefully scoop out the fruit leaving the shell intact. Trim out the tough core, cut the fruit into bite-size chunks and then toss the fruit back into the pineapple boats.

Sprinkle a bit of sugar and slop a little Grand Marnier over each half.

Serve, topped with the ice cream.

Serves: 1-2

EPT: 10 minutes

20+ WAYS TO COOK HAMBURGER

"Meat me tonight by the light of the moon"

"Noel Coward" Culpepper

Uncle Frank "Cereal" Culpepper's Hamburger Heaven Song of the Railroad:

> Burger babies come alive
> From bistro down to greasy dive.
> Cute little buns and sauces, too . . .
> Round or square or in a stew,
> Greek ones, meek ones, Sloppy Joes . . .
> How many combos? Nobody knows!
> Feeling lonely? Feeling blue?
> Grab a burger and . . . chew-chew-chew!

(I told you it was a railroad poem!)

20+ WAYS
TO COOK HAMBURGER

BACHELOR BURGER

½ lb.	ground beef	250 g
2 tsp.	finely chopped onion	10 mL
dash	garlic salt	dash
¼ tsp.	salt	1 mL
dash	pepper	dash
1	egg	1

Dump all ingredients in a bowl and mix together. Form a good-sized patty. (Remember, the burgers shrink while cooking, unless you buy lean ground beef!)

Put 1-2 tbsp. (15-30 mL) of cooking oil in a frying pan and put it on the burner at medium heat. **Little Rosie Culpepper suggests: "The medium heat is important. High heat leaves a burger black on the outside and red on the inside."**

Add ingredients and fry for approximately 7-10 minutes. Flip burger over and fry for another 7-10 minutes or until the meat is thoroughly cooked.

Serve with your favorite sauces and relishes. Add mushrooms or green peppers for something a little different.

Yield: 1 man-sized burger

EPT: 20 minutes

... AND SEVEN VARIATIONS

Chili Cheese Burgers . . . . Add ½ cup (125 mL) grated cheese, 2 tsp. (10 mL) milk and ¼ tsp. (1 mL) chili powder to the basic recipe.

Dill Burgers . . . . Add ⅛ tsp. (0.5 mL) crushed dill seed and 2 tsp.(10 mL) chopped olives OR, for a sweeter approach, add 2 tsp. (10 mL) sweet mixed pickles.

Herb Burgers . . . . Add ⅛ tsp. (0.5 mL) marjoram, a dash of thyme, ⅛ tsp. (0.5 mL) celery salt to the basic recipe.

Oriental Burgers . . . . Add ⅛ tsp. (0.5 mL) ginger, ½ tsp. (2 mL) grated lemon peel and ½ tsp. (2 mL) soy sauce to the basic recipe.

Pepper Burgers . . . . Soak 2 tsp. (10 mL) crushed peppercorns in a small bowl of cold water for 5 minutes. Drain, then add to the basic recipe.

Savory Burgers . . . . Add ⅛ tsp. (0.5 mL) savory seasoning to the basic recipe.

Sesame Burgers . . . . Turn oven to 350°F (180°C). Place 2 tsp. (10 mL) of sesame seeds in an oven-proof dish in the oven for 10-15 minutes. Add to the basic recipe.

38

SALISBURY STEAKS

½ lb.	ground beef	250 g
½	onion, diced	½
dash	salt	dash
dash	pepper	dash
dash	garlic powder	dash
3	eggs	3
1	onion, sliced	1
1 cup	beef gravy (1 pkg. prepared according to package directions)	250 mL

Toss the ground beef, diced onion, salt, pepper, garlic powder and 1 egg only in a bowl. Mix together thoroughly and shape into 2 patties. Fry these little burger babies on medium heat for about 10 minutes.

While the patties cook, add an entire sliced onion to same pan and fry it until golden brown. In another small pan, heat the gravy according to instructions on package.

When the meat patties and onion are cooked, drain the excess grease from the frying pan and then dump the gravy into the pan and let this entire preparation simmer.

While our patties simmer, take another frying pan and fry 2 eggs sunny side up.

Place the patties on dinner plates, pour the onion gravy over them, and top each with a fried egg.

Serves: 1-2

EPT: 15 minutes

CHUCKWAGONS

(Also known as "poor man's filets".)

¾ lb.	ground beef	340 g
1	egg	1
¼ tsp.	salt	1 mL
dash	pepper	dash
4	bacon slices	4

Dump ground beef, egg, salt and pepper into a medium-size bowl. Mix well, using hands (or Hans, if he's there). Shape the beef into 4 small patties, approximately 3 oz. (85 g) each. Flatten them slightly, and then wrap a half a slice of bacon around the outside rim of each patty. Secure the bacon with a toothpick.

Heat frying pan on medium heat and fry patties 5-7 minutes on each side or until done to your personal taste. Remove the toothpicks and serve with your favorite BBQ sauce.

Serves: 1-2

EPT: 20 minutes

GREEK MEATBALLS

½ lb.	ground beef	250 g
¼ cup	bread crumbs	50 mL
½ tsp.	salt	2 mL
½	onion, finely chopped	½
½ tsp.	garlic powder	2 mL
½ tsp.	dried mint	2 mL
1	egg	1
2 tsp.	ouzo OR anisette*	10 mL
2 tsp.	flour	10 mL
2 tbsp.	vegetable oil	30 mL

Mix the meat, bread crumbs, salt, onion, garlic, mint, egg and ouzo (or anisette) together in a bowl. Form into meatballs . . . like packing mudballs . . . then roll them in flour.

Heat the oil in a frying pan at medium heat and fry the meatballs until done**. The meat will turn to a brownish color. (You may develop a sudden urge to fly to Athens.)

Serves: 1-2

EPT: 20 minutes

*Thanacropolis Culpepper reminds you that ouzo and anisette are aniseed (licorice-flavored) liqueurs, available at your liquor store.

**Cousin Jeremiah Culpepper says, "However you spell ouzo, it's still Greek to me. All I know is if you're as tired of scrubbing grease spatters as I am, meatballs may also be browned in the oven, on a cookie sheet, at 400°F (200°C) for 20-25 minutes. Turn the meatballs over after 10 minutes."

PORCUPINE MEATBALLS

¾ lb.	ground beef	350 g
¼ cup	raw rice	50 mL
1	egg	1
½	small onion, diced	½
½ tsp.	salt	2 mL
dash	pepper	dash
2 tbsp.	flour	30 mL
1 tbsp.	vegetable oil	15 mL
10 oz.	tomato soup (straight from can)	284 mL
¼ cup	water	50 mL

Sling the meat, rice, egg, onion and seasonings together in a bowl. Mix thoroughly and then shape the concoction into small balls. Roll each meatball in flour.

Heat the vegetable oil in a frying pan over medium heat and fry these little critters until fully browned. Drain off the excess grease . . . leaving the meatballs in the pan.

Combine the soup and water and pour over the meatballs. Stir the meatballs around in this mixture. Let this preparation simmer, covered, for 20-30 minutes, stirring occasionally, until the rice is tender.

Serves: 1-2

EPT: 45 minutes

41

MORNING HARVEST MEAT LOAF

¾ lb.	ground beef	350 g
¼ cup	bread crumbs	50 mL
2 tsp.	ketchup	10 mL
1	egg	1
¼ tsp.	salt	1 mL
dash	sage	dash
¼ cup	applesauce	50 mL

Heat oven to 350°F (180°C).

Fling all the ingredients except applesauce into a bowl and mix lightly, using a fork. Pack down in a loaf pan and shape it any way you like . . . be creative but don't risk arrest.

Bake in oven for approximately 45 minutes and brush with applesauce just before serving.

Serves: 1-2

EPT: 50 minutes

SAUCY MEAT LOAF

1	small onion, sliced	1
¾ lb.	ground beef	350 g
1	egg	1
¼ tsp.	salt	1 mL
¼ tsp.	basil	1 mL
dash	oregano flakes	dash
10 oz.	tomato sauce (straight from can)	284 mL

Heat the oven to 375°F (190°F).

Place the onion slices in the bottom of a loaf pan.

Mix all remaining ingredients, except for the tomato sauce, in a bowl. Pack this mixture over the onions in the loaf pan.

Pour the tomato sauce over the entire preparation and bake in the oven for 45 minutes.

Serves: 1-2

EPT: 50 minutes

CHILI CON CARNE

1	onion, diced	1
½	green pepper, diced	½
¾ lb.	ground beef	350 g
handful	mushrooms, sliced	handful
⅛ tsp.	garlic powder	0.5 mL
1 cup	canned crushed tomatoes	250 mL
1 tsp.	chili powder	5 mL
dash	salt	dash
dash	pepper	dash

Fry the onion, mushrooms, and green pepper with the ground beef on medium-high heat until the beef is a light brown.

Add the remaining ingredients and simmer at low heat for 15-20 minutes.

Serves: 1

EPT: 25 minutes

...AND TWO VARIATIONS

Chili with Beans................ Add ½ cup (125 mL) canned kidney beans and ½ cup (125 mL) canned brown beans to the Chili Con Carne recipe.

Chili with Cheese.............. After the Chili Con Carne has been simmering for 15 minutes, pour the entire masterpiece into a casserole dish, sprinkle the top with grated Cheddar cheese and broil under high heat in the oven for an additional 5 minutes or until the cheese melts, then top with chopped green onions.

43

HOBBLEY COBBLEY

½ lb.	ground beef	250 g
1	onion, diced	1
dash	salt	dash
dash	pepper	dash
dash	garlic powder	dash
10 oz.	tomato soup (straight from can)	284 mL
1 cup	cooked macaroni (½ cup [125 mL] uncooked)	250 mL

Fry ground beef and onion until brown. Toss in the salt, pepper and garlic and continue to fry for 2 minutes. Then dump in the tomato soup and cooked macaroni.

Simmer for another 10 minutes, then serve.

Serves: 1-2

EPT: 25 minutes

SPICY SLOPPY JOES

½ lb.	ground beef	250 g
1 cup	pork 'n' beans (straight from can)	250 mL
½ cup	BBQ sauce	125 mL
1	green pepper, diced	1

Brown the beef and green pepper in a frying pan over medium heat for approximately 10 minutes. Now add the beans and BBQ sauce. Drain off grease.

Cook, stirring frequently, until this grand design is bubbly hot. Serve over warmed or toasted hamburger buns.

Serves: 1-2

EPT: 15 minutes

44

HAMBURGER CABBAGE LAYER

½ lb.	ground beef	250 g
dash	salt	dash
dash	pepper	dash
¼	cabbage, shredded	¼
2	potatoes, peeled and thinly sliced	2
10 oz.	cream of mushroom soup (straight from can)	284 mL
½ cup	milk	125 mL

Heat oven to 375°F (190°C).

Fry ground beef for about 10 minutes. Take (or have your dinner guest take) an occasional nibble of beef and then sprinkle with salt and pepper to season the meat to your own (or your guest's) personal taste.

Chuck a layer of ground beef into a casserole dish. Spread some shredded cabbage on top, and pop on a few potato slices as well. Continue to layer beef then cabbage then potato until all the grub is used up. Combine the soup and milk and heap over the top of this hodge-podge.

Bake, covered, in the oven for 1 hour.

Serves: 1-2

EPT: 80 minutes

CABBAGE ROLLS

½ lb.	ground beef	250 g
1 tsp.	uncooked rice	5 mL
½	onion, diced	½
dash	garlic powder	dash
dash	salt	dash
dash	pepper	dash
6	large cabbage leaves	6 large
¾ cup	tomato juice	175 mL

Heat oven to 375°F (190°C).

Combine the first 6 ingredients in a bowl. Mix well and set aside.

Boil some water in a pot. Cook the cabbage leaves for 3 minutes in the boiling water. Remove the leaves and let them cool.

Divide the beef filling into 6 portions. Take each cabbage leaf and roll a portion of the beef filling in it. Put the rolls in a casserole dish. Dump the tomato juice over the rolls, cover and bake in oven for 30-40 minutes.

Serves: 1-2

EPT: 45 minutes

45

SHEPHERD'S PIE

1	medium carrot, cleaned and sliced	1
½	onion, peeled and sliced	½
½ lb.	ground beef	250 g
¼ cup	frozen peas	50 mL
dash	salt	dash
dash	pepper	dash
½ cup	beef gravy (½ pkg. prepared to package directions)	125 mL
	potatoes, cooked and mashed (see page 13 for "Mash" technique)	
2 tbsp.	melted butter	50 mL
dash	paprika	dash

Heat oven to 375°F (190°C).

Heave those carrots into a pot. Barely cover with water and boil until they are soft and confess to being vegetables all their lives (2-3 minutes). Drain the water from the pot.

Meanwhile back at the ranch, in a separate pot, boil the onion, barely covered with water, until it softens up and agrees to play on the team (about 3 minutes). Then drain water from that pot. Or, if you want to save on clean-up, you can cook carrots and onions together.

Fry the ground beef over medium heat until brown. Drain off the grease.

Combine the ground beef, vegetables (except potatoes), salt and pepper in a casserole dish. Mash together. Let 'em really get to know each other.

Heat the gravy as directed on the package. You can thin it with boiling water if it's thicker than you like. Stir gravy into the mish-mash in the casserole dish.

Put the mashed potatoes in a pastry bag (or if you don't have one, just cut the corner out of a baggie). Squeeze the spuds through the bag and all over the top of this heavenly hash. Get as fancy and creative as you'd like here . . . maybe she's never seen her name printed in mashed potatoes on a shepherd's pie before! If you prefer, forget the pastry bag and just pile the mashed potatoes over the top and spread them as evenly as possible, or use a fork to make a pattern.

Brush the butter over the mashed potatoes. Sprinkle paprika over the surface. Bake in the oven for 20-30 minutes.

Then . . . imagine yourself out on a hillside dreaming of the little lass back at your little thatched cottage. Pretend your dinner partner is Little Bo Peep and help her find her sheep.

Serves: 1-2

EPT: 60 minutes

Fat Freddie Culpepper used to say, "Men who go on diets and swear off drinking and heavy eating for fourteen days . . . lose two weeks of precious eating and drinking time."

STUFFED PEPPERS

4	green bell peppers	4
¾ lb.	ground beef	350 g
2 tbsp.	uncooked rice	30 mL
½	onion, diced	½
dash	salt	dash
dash	pepper	dash
dash	garlic powder	dash
dash	oregano	dash
1 cup	tomato sauce	250 mL
¾ cup	grated mozzarella cheese	175 mL

Heat oven to 375°F (190°C).

Cut the tops off the peppers (like a Halloween pumpkin) and remove all the seeds from inside. Boil enough water to cover the peppers. Then drop those peppers into the boiling water and cook for 2 minutes.

Combine the ground beef, rice, onion, salt, pepper, garlic powder, and oregano. Mash them all together until they are thoroughly acquainted.

Stuff the mash mixture into the peppers. Stand the stuffed peppers in a casserole dish and dump the tomato sauce over them.

Cover with foil and bake in oven for approximately 40 minutes. Uncover and top with the grated cheese 5 minutes before the end of cooking.

Serves: 1-2

EPT: 60 minutes

NOTE: **There's no law against experimenting with your own spicy meat concoctions. But do the world a favor and try the little masterpieces yourself before sharing them with a cynical public ... or a special guest!**

47

GROUND BEEF 'N' GREENS

½ lb.	ground beef	250 g
2	celery stalks, sliced	2
1 cup	broccoli, sliced	250 mL
½	onion, diced	½
1	carrot, thinly sliced	1
1 cup	beef bouillon	250 mL
3 tbsp.	cornstarch	45 mL
½ cup	cold water	125 mL
2 tsp.	soy sauce	10 mL
	salt, to taste	
	pepper, to taste	

Fry ground beef until brown. Add celery, broccoli, onion, carrots and bouillon. Continue to cook, stirring regularly, for 4-5 minutes, until vegetables are tender-crisp. Keep this mixture simmering.

Add cornstarch to the water and mix until the mess is sticky and pasty looking. Add small dollops of the cornstarch mixture into the bubbling main mass of meat and vegetables until you get your own desired thickness. You may not have to use the entire amount. Let this situation simmer for another 2 minutes. Then flip in the soy sauce, salt and pepper. Give the concoction one last swirl and serve . . . as Ground Beef 'N' Greens.

Serves: 1-2

EPT: 25 minutes

GROUND BEEF STEW

½ lb.	ground beef	250 g
½	onion, diced	½
1	carrot, diced	1
2	celery stalks, diced	2
handful	mushrooms, sliced	handful
dash	salt	dash
dash	pepper	dash
1 cup	beef gravy (1 pkg. cooked to directions on package)	250 mL

Fry ground beef, celery, mushrooms and onion on medium heat until brown. This takes about 10 minutes.

Meanwhile, pitch those carrots into a separate pot, barely cover them with water and boil until they soften up, (2-3 minutes).

Sling the cooked carrots and spices into the main pan. Throw in the gravy and simmer for another 10 minutes.

Serves: 1-2

EPT: 25 minutes

CHEESY BEEF CARBONNADE

1 tbsp.	butter	15 mL
½	onion, diced	½
½ lb.	ground beef	250 g
2 tbsp.	all-purpose flour	30 mL
6 oz.	beer (½ bottle)	170 mL
1	potato, boiled and cubed	1
½ cup	sliced mushrooms,	125 mL
2 tsp.	tomato paste	10 mL
¼ tsp.	Worcestershire sauce	1 mL
	salt and pepper, to taste	
⅓ cup	grated Cheddar cheese	75 mL
¼ cup	grated Parmesan cheese	50 mL
1 tsp.	chopped parsley (optional)	5 mL

Melt butter in a medium frying pan. Add onion and ground beef. Fry, stirring gently for 5-10 minutes or until cooked.

Stir in flour, beer, potato, mushrooms, tomato purée, Worcestershire, salt and pepper. Put on high heat until the concoction boils. Then lower heat to simmer and let the beast simmer down for 25-30 minutes. Drink the other half of the beer before the fizz disappears.

Sprinkle Carbonnade with cheeses and parsley (if you like) and serve on a hot platter. (Scrumptious when served with a tossed green salad.)

Serves: 1-2

EPT: 45 minutes

GROUND BEEF STROGANOFF

½ lb.	ground beef	250 g
¼	onion, diced	¼
handful	mushrooms, sliced	handful
¼ tsp.	paprika	1 mL
dash	salt	dash
dash	pepper	dash
1 cup	beef gravy (1 pkg. cooked to pkg. directions)	250 mL
4 tbsp.	sour cream	60 mL
1	dill pickle, diced	1

Fry the ground beef and onion on medium heat for 5 minutes. Mix in mushrooms and continue to fry until the grub browns up. Fling in the paprika, salt and pepper and continue to cook for 2 minutes. Then dump in the gravy and simmer for another 5 minutes. Just before serving, stir in the sour cream and dill pickle and heat through*.

Serves: 1-2

EPT: 20 minutes

*Anastasia Culpepper, who came to this country after her Czar broke down, always encouraged us to serve this masterpiece over cooked buttered noodles. So eat and enjoy and sing several Russian folk songs for dessert.

49

LASAGNE

6	lasagne noodles	6
½ lb.	ground beef	250 g
½	onion, diced	½
2	celery stalks, diced	2
1	carrot, finely diced	1
handful	mushrooms, sliced	handful
¼ tsp.	garlic powder	1 mL
dash	salt	dash
dash	pepper	dash
¼ tsp.	Italian seasoning	1 mL
1 cup	tomato sauce	250 mL
1 cup	grated mozzarella cheese (4 oz. [115 g]	250 mL

Heat oven to 375°F (190°C).

Cook the noodles according to the package directions and then place to the side.

Fry ground beef, onion, celery, carrots, mushrooms and seasonings on medium heat for 10 minutes. Then add the tomato sauce and simmer for 15 minutes. (Just the sauce . . . hold that cheese!)

Place 2 lasagne noodles in the bottom of a 1-quart (1 L) casserole dish or loaf pan. Dump half of the meat mixture on top. Spread it evenly over the noodles. Cover this layer with 2 more noodles. Then a layer of meat again. Place the final 2 noodles over the second layer of meat. Now sprinkle the grated cheese over the top layer of noodles.

Bake this Italian masterpiece in the oven for 20 minutes.

Serves: 1-2

EPT: 45 minutes

. . . AND FOUR VARIATIONS

Creamy Lasagne . . . . Add a thin layer of creamy cottage cheese between the 2 noodle/meat layers.

Lasagne Florentine . . . . Cook ½ package (5 oz. [140 g]) frozen spinach, then add a thin layer between the 2 noodle/meat layers.

Ukrainian Lasagne . . . . Add thin slices of kohbasa between the 2 noodle/meat layers.

Vegetarian Lasagne . . . . Forget the ground beef!! Replace with your favorite vegetables . . . diced into tasty bite-sized chunks.

SPAGHETTI AND MEAT SAUCE

½ lb.	ground beef	250 g
½	onion, diced	½
handful	mushrooms, sliced	handful
dash	salt	dash
dash	pepper	dash
dash	garlic powder	dash
1 cup	tomato sauce	250 mL
	spaghetti (any amount . . . 2 equal portions)	

Fry ground beef and onions on medium heat for about 5 minutes. Add mushrooms and continue to fry until it browns up. Sling in the salt, pepper and garlic powder. Now dump in the tomato sauce. Simmer for 10 minutes.

Meanwhile, with your other 2 hands, cook the spaghetti according to the directions on the package.

When both parties are ready, have them meet in the middle of your plate and try not to drip any on your shirt . . . unless your shirt is already the color of the tomato sauce. In other words, dump the meat sauce over the spaghetti and serve.

Serves: 1-2

EPT: 30 minutes

Uncle Horace Culpepper's Advice to the Lovelorn: A young man with his first cigar makes himself sick. A young man with his first love makes everybody sick.

POOR MAN'S POTLUCK

Mary Elizabeth "I've got more kids than brains" Culpepper once remarked: Say what you will about "puttin' on the Ritz", there are days when both cupboard and imagination are bare! At such times. . .

> Haul out the campfire wieners and beans
> A poor man's potluck is just what it seems
> With liver and onions or mulligan stew
> Or tacos or pizza — macaroni will do!
> Add your meatballs or sausages — any old thing
> A good poor man's potluck is fit for a king.

POOR MAN'S POTLUCK

CAMPFIRE WIENERS AND BEANS

3	wieners (hot dogs)	3
10 oz.	pork 'n' beans (1 can)	284 mL
1 tbsp.	ketchup	15 mL
2 tsp.	brown sugar	10 mL

Cut the wieners into 1" (2.5 cm) slices and boil for 3 minutes. In another pot, heat the pork 'n' beans on medium heat. Throw in the ketchup and brown sugar, then the wieners. Stir them around a bit, simmer for 2 minutes, and serve immediately.

Serves: 1-2

EPT: 15 minutes

EGGS IN THE HOLE

3	slices French bread, 1" (2.5 cm) thick	3
3 tsp.	butter	15 mL
3	eggs	3
	salt and pepper, to taste	

Butter both sides of each slice of bread. Then tear a hole in the center of the bread, or cut one out with a small glass.

Plop the bread in the pan. Plunk 1 tsp. (15 mL) of butter into the hole on each slice of bread. When butter bubbles crack an egg into the center. Season eggs with salt and pepper.

Let 'em cook for a few minutes until the underside of the bread is brown. Then flip the little fellows over and brown the other side.

Great with ketchup!

Serves: 1-2

EPT: 15 minutes

HAM AND POTATO STEW

2	medium potatoes, peeled, diced in 1" (2.5 cm) pieces	2
½ lb.	ham, diced in ½" (1.5 cm) pieces	250 g
2	green onions, diced	2
	salt and pepper, to taste	
1 tbsp.	butter	15 mL

Fling potato pieces into a pot, barely cover them with water and boil until tender, about 15 minutes.

Drain off half the liquid. Dump the ham into the cooked potatoes. Splash some salt and pepper over the concoction. Simmer on stove until remaining juice has thickened and the stew is piping hot. Garnish with green onions and spread butter over before serving.

Serves: 1-2   *EPT:* 25 minutes

LIVER AND ONIONS

1 tbsp.	butter	15 mL
	salt and pepper, to taste	
¾ lb.	liver, sliced	350 g
½ cup	flour	125 mL
1	onion, thinly sliced	1

Melt butter in frying pan. Pour the flour onto a plate. Throw some salt and pepper over the liver then drop the liver in the flour. Roll it around a bit and then plop the liver into frying pan and let it cook for 2 minutes over medium-high heat.

Turn liver over, toss in the onion slices and continue frying the liver, with the onions, for another 2 minutes.

Optional: A little brown gravy adds a bit of moisture.

Serves: 1-2

EPT: 10 minutes

MULLIGAN STEW

¾ cup	uncooked macaroni	175 mL
6.5 oz	can flaked tuna	184 g
10 oz.	can cream of celery soup	284 mL
	salt and pepper, to taste	

Cook macaroni according to the instructions on the package. Drain the macaroni and return it to the pot. Drain the liquid off the tuna. Scoop the tuna and soup together into the macaroni. Add salt and pepper to your own personal taste. Mix it around a bit, heat on low for a few minutes and serve.

Serves: 1-2

EPT: 20 minutes

TOMATO MACARONI

¾ cup	uncooked macaroni	175 mL
¾ cup	canned whole tomatoes, drained	175 mL
½ cup	tomato soup (straight from can)	125 mL
	salt and pepper, to taste	

Cook macaroni according to instructions on package. Drain and put back in the pot.

Cut the whole tomatoes into bite-sized pieces. Toss the tomato pieces, tomato soup and some salt and pepper into the macaroni. Mix and serve piping hot.

Serves: 1-2

EPT: 20 minutes

MEATBALLS IN MUSHROOM SAUCE

1 lb.	ground beef	500 g
½ tsp.	salt	2 mL
¼ tsp.	pepper	1 mL
1	egg	1
10 oz.	can cream of mushroom soup	284 mL
¼ cup	flour	50 mL

Mash beef, salt, pepper and egg together in a bowl. Hack out and shape 8 meatballs and roll them in flour.

On a medium-low burner, fry meatballs about 15 minutes. Drain off excess grease. Slosh the soup over the meatballs and simmer for another 5 minutes. Serve with rice.

Serves: 1-2

EPT: 20 minutes

STUFFED TACOS

¾ lb.	ground beef	350 g
½	onion, diced	½
½ tsp.	salt	2 mL
¼ tsp.	pepper	1 mL
dash	chili powder	dash
4	taco shells	4
1	tomato, diced	1
¼	head lettuce, shredded	¼
½ cup	grated Cheddar cheese	125 mL
	hot sauce for tacos	

Fry beef and onion on medium heat until golden brown. Season with salt, pepper and chili. Stuff cooked beef into taco shells. Top with tomato and lettuce, then sprinkle grated cheese over it and serve with hot sauce. Lean back and dream of Pancho Villa.

Serves: 1-2

EPT: 25 minutes

PITA PIZZA

1	piece pita bread OR as many as required	1
¼ cup	pizza sauce	50 mL
½ cup	grated mozzarella cheese (2 oz. [55 g])	125 mL
	any pizza toppings, to taste	

Heat oven to 350°F (180°C).

Make a slit near edge of pita bread. Place the firm side of pita down on a baking sheet. Stuff pizza sauce, cheese and your favorite toppings into the pita pocket. Place on a tray in the oven and cook until the sauce and cheese inside the pita are bubbling.

Serves: 1-2

EPT: 15 minutes

RICE-BASED PIZZA

3 cups	cooked rice	750 mL
2	eggs, beaten	2
2 cups	grated mozzarella cheese	500 mL
1 tsp.	oregano	5 mL
¼ tsp.	salt	1 mL
¼ tsp.	garlic powder	1 mL
¾ cup	tomato sauce	175 mL
1	green pepper, sliced	1
	toppings of pepperoni, pineapple, etc.	

Mix the rice, eggs and 1 cup (250 mL) of the cheese. Put this mixture into a greased frying pan. Cover it. Cook at medium-low for 15 minutes. This rice base is your crust.

The crust should be slightly brown and beginning to set. Combine oregano, salt, garlic powder and tomato sauce to make the sauce. Prepare the toppings. Spread the sauce on the base. Top with green pepper and add toppings of your choice. Sprinkle the other 1 cup (250 mL) of cheese over the sauce. Cover and cook 10 minutes at the same heat.

Uncover and cook for an additional 5 minutes.

Serves: 1-2

EPT: 30 minutes

SPANISH SAUSAGES

8	beef OR pork sausages	8
1 tbsp.	vegetable oil	15 mL
1 cup	canned whole tomatoes	250 mL
½	onion, diced	½
½	green pepper, diced	½
½ tsp.	salt	2 mL
¼ tsp.	pepper	1 mL
½ tsp.	garlic salt	2 mL

Fry sausages in oil for approximately 15 minutes on medium heat . . . browning on all sides. Meanwhile, cut tomatoes into smaller bite-sized pieces. (Save the juice.) Set aside.

Dump the onion, green pepper and seasonings in with the sausages and continue to cook for 5 minutes. Then drain the oil from the pan and slosh the tomatoes and juice over the sausages.

Let the entire messterpiece come to a boil and then simmer for a further 5 minutes before serving.

Serves: 1-2

EPT: 30 minutes

CAREER-PATH CASSEROLES

Cousin Virginia Raphael Culpepper of Schneiderville declares: "The advantage in making a casserole is that the positive flavors of the proper ingredients often outweigh the negative flavors of the wrong ingredients. There is room to experiment. Of course, the disadvantage of these exercises is that if your special dish turns out to be the "hit of the party", it's often difficult to tell why . . . or remember how you did it. These "all-in-one-pot" meals are easy to prepare, simple to serve, leave a little slack for fun, and, if necessary, can feed an army or the entire softball team."

CAREER-PATH CASSEROLES

BAKED ROTINI

1½ cups	uncooked rotini pasta, cooked	375 mL
1 cup	spaghetti sauce	250 mL
¼ cup	grated mozzarella cheese	50 mL

Heat oven to 375°F (190°C).

Dump the rotini pasta and spaghetti sauce into a casserole dish. Stir to combine.

Bake, covered, in oven for 20 minutes.

Remove lid and sprinkle the cheese over the top. Then continue to bake, uncovered, for another 10 minutes.

Serves: 1-2

EPT: 40 minutes

MACARONI AND CHEESE

1 cup	uncooked long macaroni, cooked*	250 mL
¼ cup	diced ham	50 mL
1 cup	grated Cheddar cheese (4 oz. [115 g])	250 mL
½ cup	milk	125 mL
dash	onion powder	dash
¼ tsp.	salt	1 mL
dash	pepper	dash
¼ cup	bread crumbs	50 mL

Heat oven to 375°F (190°C).

Throw the macaroni, ham, cheese, milk, onion powder, salt and pepper into a casserole dish. Stir to combine. Cover and bake in oven for 25 minutes, stirring occasionally.

Remove the cover and sprinkle the bread crumbs on top and return, uncovered, to the oven to brown. Bake for another 10 minutes.

Serves: 1

EPT: 25 minutes

*Dr. Diogenes Culpepper recommends: Measure the raw macaroni in the cup ... then cook that amount!

CHICKEN À LA KING

1 tsp.	butter	5 mL
1	small green pepper, chopped	1
handful	mushrooms, sliced	handful
dash	salt	dash
dash	pepper	dash
1½ cups	chopped cooked chicken OR turkey	375 mL
10 oz.	can cream of chicken soup	284 mL
¼ cup	milk	50 mL

Heat oven to 375°F (190°C).

Melt butter in frying pan over low heat. Fling in the green peppers and mushrooms and fry until tender . . . but DO NOT brown. Dash your salt and pepper over the veggies.

Drain off oil.

Throw these veggies and all remaining ingredients into a casserole dish. Stir well.

Bake, covered, in oven for 20 minutes.

Can be served over toast, rice or noodles.

Serves: 1-2

EPT: 30 minutes

CHICKEN POT PIE

1½ cups	chopped cooked chicken	375 mL
10 oz.	cream of chicken soup (straight from can)	284 mL
½ cup	frozen mixed vegetables, defrosted	125 mL
¼ cup	milk	50 mL
dash	pepper	dash
4	bread slices, cubed	4
2 tsp.	butter, melted	10 mL

Heat oven to 375°F (190°C).

Heave the chicken, soup, vegetables, milk and pepper into a casserole dish. Stir well. Pop the lid on top and place in the oven. Let bake for 20 minutes, stirring occasionally.

Meanwhile, mix the bread cubes in the melted butter.

Remove casserole from oven and drop the bread cubes over the concoction to form a crust. Bake, uncovered, for another 10 minutes, then serve.

Serves: 1-2

EPT: 30 minutes

CORNED BEEF AND CABBAGE

1	large potato, thinly sliced	1
1	small onion, sliced	1
2 tbsp.	water	30 mL
dash	salt	dash
dash	pepper	dash
½ lb.	corned beef, shredded	250 g
¼	head cabbage, cut into small wedges	¼
2 tbsp.	butter, melted	30 mL

Heat oven to 375°F (190°C).

In a greased casserole dish, layer potato slices and onions. Add water, salt and pepper. Cover and bake in oven for 20 minutes.

Place the cabbage wedges evenly over the potatoes and sprinkle corned beef over them. Pour the butter over. Cover and continue to bake for an additional 15 minutes.

Serves: 1-2

EPT: 40 minutes

COUNTRY HAM CASSEROLE

1 cup	uncooked macaroni, cooked	250 mL
1 cup	chopped cooked ham	250 mL
1 cup	grated Swiss cheese	250 mL
⅔ cup	cream of celery soup (straight from the can)	150 mL
1 cup	green peas, drained, canned OR frozen	250 mL
¼ cup	milk	50 mL
1 tsp.	Dijon mustard	5 mL
¼ cup	crushed corn chips	50 mL

Heat oven to 375°F (190°C).

Dump the macaroni, ham, ½ of the Swiss cheese, soup, peas, milk and mustard into a casserole dish and swirl this interesting arrangement around.

Throw a lid on the dish and bake this aromatic aggregation in the oven for 20 minutes, stirring occasionally.

Remove from the oven and sprinkle the remaining cheese and corn chips over the top and serve.

Serves: 1-2

EPT: 60 minutes

LATE NIGHT SUPPER

1 cup	grated Cheddar cheese	250 mL
2	bacon slices, diced	2
¼ cup	onion, diced	50 mL
10 oz.	cream of celery soup (straight from the can)	284 mL
⅓ cup	water	75 mL
2	large cooked potatoes, sliced	2
handful	mushrooms, sliced	handful
1 cup	chopped cooked chicken	250 mL

Heat oven to 325°F (160°C).

Fry the bacon and onions on medium heat until cooked. Drain off excess grease.

Pour the soup right from the can over the bacon and onions and add the water. Stir well.

Heave the potatoes, mushrooms and chicken into the frying pan. Push 'em around a bit, then dump the entire works into a casserole dish. Top with cheese. Bake, uncovered, in oven for 25 minutes.

Serves: 1-2

EPT: 30 minutes

MEXICAN MELODY

½ lb.	ground beef	250 g
½	onion, chopped	½
1 cup	tomato sauce	250 mL
½ cup	kernel corn	125 mL
1 cup	uncooked pasta sea shells, cooked	250 mL
½ tsp.	chili powder	2 mL
handful	taco chips	handful

Heat oven to 375°F (190°C).

Fry ground beef and onions on medium heat until brown. Dump in the tomato sauce, kernel corn, sea shells and chili powder. Mix it all up and then plop the whole mess into a casserole dish.

Bake, covered, in oven for 25 minutes.

Stand the taco chips on top and serve.

Serves: 1-2

EPT: 35 minutes

ITALIAN SAUSAGE

¾ lb.	spicy, Italian sausage, cut in 1½" (4 cm) slices	350 g
2	small green peppers, cubed	2
1	carrot, sliced	1
1 cup	Rotini noodles raw (cooked)	250 mL
dash	garlic salt	dash
1	onion, cubed	1
1 cup	tomato sauce	250 mL
¼ tsp.	salt	1 mL
¼ tsp.	oregano	1 mL
dash	pepper	dash

Heat oven to 375°F (190°C).

Slash the sausages with a knife. Catapult the sausages, green peppers, carrot and garlic into a casserole dish. Cover the dish before they escape and throw it into oven for 20 minutes. Stir occasionally while baking.

Fling in the remaining ingredients, cover, and continue to bake for 20 minutes or until vegetables are tender.

Serves: 1-2

EPT: 50 minutes

TUNA CASSEROLE

4 oz.	can flaked tuna, drained	113 g
½ cup	uncooked macaroni, cooked, drained	125 mL
½	can cream of celery soup	142 mL
handful	mushrooms, sliced	handful
1 cup	frozen peas	250 mL
¼ cup	milk	50 mL
1 cup	crushed sour cream 'n' onion potato chips	250 mL

Heat oven to 375° (190°C).

Dump the tuna, macaroni, soup, mushrooms, peas and milk into a 1-quart (1 L) casserole dish. Slosh it all together.

Cover and bake in oven for 25 minutes, stirring occasionally.

Top with potato chips and serve.

Serves: 1-2

EPT: 45 minutes

ZUCCHINI PARMESAN

6 slices	ham, sliced in thin strips	6 slices
2	small zucchini, sliced ¼" (0.5 cm) thick	2
1 tbsp.	butter, melted	15 mL
2 cups	spaghetti sauce	500 mL
1 cup	grated mozzarella cheese	250 mL
2 tbsp.	grated Parmesan cheese	30 mL
¼ cup	bread crumbs	50 mL

Heat oven to 375°F (190°C).

Plop ham and zucchini slices into casserole dish. Pour melted butter over the top. Cover and throw into oven for 10 minutes.

Fling the spaghetti sauce into the mess and continue to bake, covered, for an additional 20 minutes.

Remove lid. Sprinkle cheeses and bread crumbs over the top.

Bake, uncovered, for another 10 minutes, then serve.

Serves: 1-2

EPT: 30 minutes

Joanne Maree (PhD) Culpepper's Helpful Household Hint #143:

Casseroles are complete meals in a dish with the meat, veggies, sauce and whatever else is necessary all thrown together. But, remember, just because more than half the accidents in the home happen in the kitchen that's no reason for you to force yourself and your date to eat them. You can always go out to that little fast food place around the corner. (Mind you, that could be just as dangerous!)

OH WOW! NOT THE FLYING ZUCCHINI BROTHERS?

MICROWAVE COOKING

Remember the first time you drove the car to school on your own? Some of us never wanted to walk again! That's how some guys feel when they catch on to microwave cooking. The microwave is to cooking what Elvis was to classical music . . . all shook up, unpopular with traditionalists, and the darling of the younger crowd.

If cooking is a chore to you, consider buying a microwave oven. It will heat casseroles, defrost frozen foods, cook up a great hot dog, reheat leftovers and warm up beverages faster and more easily than you have ever seen.

If cooking is a pleasure to you, consider buying a microwave oven. Your results will be as tasty as when prepared by more conventional means but will take about one-third of the time and give you a chance to entertain your dinner guest or enjoy your own private drink before dinner.

A few things to remember when using a microwave oven:

* Microwave cooking is best for small to medium quantities of food. Large roasts, turkeys or lots of potatoes are better prepared in a conventional oven.

* Use only containers and utensils designed to let microwave energy pass through them. Most will be marked for microwave use.

* Microwaves are not good for eggs in the shell . . . and vice versa. (The eggs will cook . . . but will also explode!)

* Chicken, steak and chops won't have the crispy outer crust that you get when broiling or frying them.

* When using plastic wrap (as called for in some of our recipes) make sure that it is "microwave safe". It should be labelled as such on the package. Never use foil.

* The speed at which certain dishes become fully cooked requires careful meal planning.

* Different microwaves have different cooking times for different amounts of food. Your microwave's cooking time may be slightly different from the times listed in the recipes in this chapter.

Taking 5 minutes to jot down a game plan for the preparation of the meal is an important task for the novice chef.

The simple calculation of when each dish needs to be started in order to be ready for a properly timed presentation of the whole meal, prevents a stress-filled session.

The disorganized cook can take the fun out of an evening for both himself and his guest(s). The organized kitchen-conqueror makes the preparation and presentation of the meal appear to be flawless.

A microwave oven saves time. But, a well-prepared cook can prevent tension and save the dining experience.

MICROWAVE COOKING

BBQ MEAT LOAF

½ lb.	hamburger	250 g
2 tbsp.	bread crumbs	30 mL
⅓ cup	milk	75 mL
1	egg	1
1 tbsp.	chopped onion	15 mL
1 tbsp.	chopped green pepper	15 mL
1 tsp.	Worcestershire sauce	5 mL
dash	salt	dash
¼ tsp.	Dijon mustard	1 mL
dash	pepper	dash
dash	ground sage	dash
4 tbsp.	BBQ sauce	60 mL

Slap all ingredients together, except half the BBQ sauce. Pack this concoction evenly in a greased micro-safe loaf pan. Now dribble the other half of the BBQ sauce over the top.

Cover with wax paper and cook on MEDIUM for 8 minutes. Turn pan around and continue to cook for another 8 minutes. Let it stand for 5, then brush the top with a bit more BBQ sauce before serving.

Serves: 1-2

EPT: 25 minutes

PATTY PIZZA

½ lb.	ground beef	250 g
1 tbsp.	finely chopped onion	15 mL
¼ tsp.	salt	1 mL
dash	ground oregano	dash
2 tbsp.	spaghetti sauce	30 mL
¼	onion, sliced	¼
¼	green pepper, sliced	¼
2	mozzarella cheese slices, cut into strips	2

Mash ground beef, onion, salt and oregano together. Shape into 2 patties, ¼" (1 cm). Pop the patties into a baking dish. Place another dish on top for weight to keep the patties flat. Heat at MEDIUM for 4 minutes, then drain off the excess liquid.

Plop spaghetti sauce, onions and green peppers on the patties and cook at MEDIUM for 2 minutes. Top with cheese, cook at MEDIUM for an additional 4 minutes. Remove and let stand, covered, for 3 minutes before serving.

Serves: 1-2

EPT: 15 minutes

ITALIAN MEATBALLS

1 cup	tomato sauce	250 mL
½ lb.	ground beef	250 g
1	egg	1
1 cup	bread crumbs	250 mL
1 tbsp.	grated Parmesan cheese	15 mL
2 tbsp.	water	30 mL
½ tsp.	oregano	2 mL
½ tsp.	parsley	2 mL
¼ cup	diced onion	50 mL

Set tomato sauce aside and pound all other ingredients together and shape into golf ball-size meatballs (about 10). Toss them into a baking dish. Pop this dish into the microwave on MEDIUM-HIGH heat and let cook for about 10 minutes.

Drain off the excess liquid. Mix in the tomato sauce with the meatballs and cook for an additional 4 minutes at MEDIUM. Let stand for another 3 minutes before serving.

Serves: 1-2

EPT: 20 minutes

ITALIAN BEEF SPAGHETTI

½ lb.	stewing beef, in ½" (1.5 cm) cubes	250 g
1 cup	spaghetti sauce	250 mL
2 tbsp.	red wine	30 mL
¼ cup	water	50 mL
¼ cup	diced green pepper	50 mL
1 tsp.	onion soup mix	5 mL
8 oz.	uncooked spaghetti, cooked	250 g
¼ cup	grated Parmesan cheese	50 mL

Fling the beef, spaghetti sauce, wine, water, green pepper and soup mix into a casserole dish. Cover and cook on HIGH for 4 minutes. Stir the concoction, then cover it again and cook at MEDIUM for 30 minutes . . . stirring every 10 minutes.

Meanwhile, in another part of the kitchen, cook the spaghetti according to the directions on the package. When the sauce is finished cooking, splash it over the spaghetti, garnish with Parmesan cheese, start to sing a sexy song in Italian and serve with a flourish.

Serves: 1-2

EPT: 40 minutes

CABBAGE ROLLS

½	small head cabbage	½
½ lb.	ground beef	250 g
½	onion, chopped	½
1 tsp.	uncooked rice	5 mL
1 tsp.	salt	5 mL
dash	pepper	dash
¼ cup	sauerkraut	50 mL
1 cup	tomato sauce	250 mL
1 tbsp.	brown sugar	15 mL
2	bacon strips, cut in half	2

Cut core from cabbage then rinse. Throw the cabbage into a medium-size bowl, cover with plastic wrap, and heat on HIGH for 1 minute.

Remove 6 leaves from cabbage.

Pound the ground beef, onions, rice, salt and pepper together. Place some of the beef-rice concoction on each of the cabbage leaves. Top each with sauerkraut. Roll the leaves up, folding edges in.

Dice the remaining cabbage and place in oblong dish. Arrange the cabbage rolls on top of this bed of diced cabbage. Slosh the tomato sauce and brown sugar together and then splash this mixture over the rolls. Lay the bacon strips on top of the cabbage rolls. Cover dish with microwave-approved plastic wrap. Heat on MEDIUM for 15-20 minutes.

Let stand, covered, for 5 minutes before serving.

Serves: 1-2

EPT: 30 minutes

SWISS STEAK

4	boneless round steaks (4 oz. [115 g])	4
1¼ cups	canned tomatoes	284 mL
½ cup	tomato sauce	125 mL
2 tbsp.	onion soup mix	30 mL
½	onion, sliced	½
½ tsp.	basil	2 mL
dash	garlic powder	dash
3	mozzarella cheese slices	3

Pound steaks until they are thin. Chop tomatoes into small pieces. Place steaks in a baking dish. Combine the tomatoes, tomato sauce, soup mix, onions, basil and garlic and dump over steaks. Throw some microwave-approved plastic wrap over the dish.

Heat at HIGH for 5 minutes, then continue to cook at LOW for another 35 minutes. Top with cheese, then let stand, covered, for 10 minutes before serving.

Serves: 1-2

EPT: 45 minutes

VEAL CORDON BLEU

2	veal cutlets (8 oz. [250 g] each)	2
1	thin ham slice	1
1	Swiss cheese slice	1
¾ cup	bread crumbs	175 mL
¼ tsp.	salt	1 mL
dash	pepper	dash
1	egg, beaten with 1 tbsp. (15 mL) milk	1
2 tbsp.	vegetable oil	30 mL
½ cup	tomato sauce	125 mL

Cut the cutlets in half, lengthwise. Pound them until they are very thin. Place half a slice of ham and half a slice of cheese on 2 of the cutlets. Put the other 2 cutlets on top of these dressed cutlets . . . making 2 cutlet sandwiches. Pound the edges together to seal or secure with wooden toothpicks.

Put these cutlets into the freezer until frozen solid.

Season bread crumbs by chucking in the salt and pepper. Dip the frozen cutlet sandwiches into the beaten egg and then into bread crumb mixture. Make sure both sides are thoroughly "crumbed".

Coat bottom of a baking dish with half of the oil. Place the cutlets in the dish. Sprinkle remaining oil over cutlets. Cover with wax paper and cook at MEDIUM-HIGH for about 6 minutes, turning cutlets over once while cooking.

Let stand for 3 minutes, covered with wax paper, before serving. While the veal is standing, heat up the tomato sauce. Pour the sauce over the veal and serve.

Serves: 1-2

EPT: 20 minutes

CHINESE PORK AND PEA PODS

½ lb.	boneless pork	250 g
1 tbsp.	vegetable oil	15 mL
¼ cup	diced onions	50 mL
1 tbsp.	soy sauce	15 mL
dash	garlic salt	dash
handful	pea pods, defrost if frozen	handful
1 tbsp.	cornstarch	15 mL
1 cup	beef broth	250 mL

Cut pork into thin strips. Heat oil in a casserole dish at MEDIUM for 1½ minutes. Stir in pork, onions, soy sauce and garlic salt. Cook at HIGH for 2-3 minutes, stirring twice.

Throw pods into dish, cover with microwave-approved plastic wrap, and cook at MEDIUM for another 2 minutes, stirring once.

Blend cornstarch with cold beef broth. Add this to the pork dish and continue to cook on HIGH for 3 minutes, stirring once more while the concoction is cooking.

Serves: 1-2

EPT: 20 minutes

FRIED PORK CHOPS

2	pork chops, ½" (1.5 cm) thick	2
½	pkg. seasoned coating mix	½
¼ cup	applesauce	50 mL

Coat pork chops according to the instructions on seasoned coating mix package. Pop chops in a baking dish (ribs towards the center). Cook at MEDIUM for 6½-8 minutes. Flip during cooking time. Let stand for 3 minutes before serving. Serve with the applesauce.

Serves: 1-2

EPT: 10 minutes

SOUTHERN RIBS

1 lb.	pork back ribs	500 g
½ cup	BBQ sauce	125 mL
1 tbsp.	honey	15 mL
1 tbsp.	flour	15 mL
2 tsp.	soy sauce	10 mL
1 tsp.	lemon juice	5 mL
¼ tsp.	garlic powder	1 mL

Slice the rib rack into individual ribs. Mix the remaining ingredients in a bowl and toss the ribs into this mixture. Slosh them around for a bit.

Place the ribs, meat-side-down, in a casserole dish. Pour remaining mixture over them. Cover dish with wax paper. Cook on HIGH for 6 minutes, turn the ribs over, and baste them with the mixture in the dish. Then cook at MEDIUM for 13 minutes. Serve with a Southern accent.

Serves: 1-2

EPT: 25 minutes

BBQ SHORT RIBS

2 lbs.	beef short ribs	1 kg
½	onion, sliced	½
1	celery stalk, sliced	1
⅔ cup	ketchup	150 mL
2 tbsp.	vinegar	30 mL
½ tsp.	Worcestershire sauce	2 mL
dash each	salt, dry mustard	dash
¼ cup	water	50 mL

Arrange ribs in a baking dish with the meatiest portions toward edge of dish. Throw in onion and celery. Cover with microwave-approved plastic wrap and cook at MEDIUM for 10 minutes.

Meanwhile, swirl the ketchup, vinegar, water, Worcestershire sauce, salt and dry mustard together in a bowl and pour this lovely sauce over the ribs.

Cover the ribs and cook at HIGH for 5 minutes. Then cook at LOW for 1 hour.

Baste ribs with sauce occasionally while cooking. Let ribs stand, covered, for 5 minutes before serving.

Serves: 1-2

EPT: 85 minutes

72

CHICKEN PARMESAN

2	small boneless chicken breasts	2
½ cup	bread crumbs	125 mL
2 tbsp.	grated Parmesan cheese	30 mL
dash each	salt and pepper	dash
¼ tsp.	poultry seasoning	1 mL
1	egg	1
2 tbsp.	flour	30 mL
1 tbsp.	vegetable oil	15 mL
1 cup	tomato sauce	250 mL

Pound chicken breasts until thin. Combine the bread crumbs, Parmesan cheese, salt, pepper and poultry seasoning. Beat that egg. Pat the chicken with flour then dip into the egg mess then into the Parmesan cheese concoction.

Pour the oil into an oblong dish and heat on MEDIUM for 1 minute. Stick the chicken into the dish and cook on MEDIUM for 2½ minutes on each side.

Remove the chicken from the microwave and let stand for 3 minutes.

Heat the tomato sauce in a bowl at MEDIUM for about 2 minutes.

Splash the heated sauce over chicken, sprinkle with additional Parmesan and serve.

Serves: 1-2

EPT: 25 minutes

MACARONI AND CHEESE

1 cup	hot water	250 mL
1 cup	uncooked macaroni	250 mL
1 tbsp.	butter	15 mL
1 tbsp.	chopped onion	15 mL
dash each	salt, pepper, dry mustard	dash
⅔ cup	milk	150 mL
1 cup	diced process cheese	250 mL
3 tbsp.	flour	45 mL
1 tbsp.	grated Parmesan cheese	15 mL

Throw water, macaroni, butter, onion, salt, pepper and mustard into a casserole dish. Cover and cook on HIGH for 3 minutes. Stir, then cover again and cook another 3 minutes on MEDIUM. Strain off the liquid.

Hurl in the remaining ingredients, except for the Parmesan cheese. Cover the dish and return to HIGH. Cook for 6-8 minutes, stirring occasionally. Sometime during the last 2 minutes, sprinkle the Parmesan cheese on top.

Serves: 1-2

EPT: 20 minutes

Grandfather Culpepper's Cavity Cure-all: When suffering from a violent toothache in a hollow tooth, fill the cavity with whiskey. Hold the whiskey there for thirty seconds, cocking your head to one side. Gulp down the whiskey and refill cavity. Repeat, until you don't give a damn whether you have a toothache or not. (Hint: You don't have to wait for a toothache to try this treatment ... but, if you drink, don't drive!)

ECONOMICALLY SERVING SEAFOOD

Aunt Elvona "Arkansas" Culpepper: The saying "There's more than one fish in the sea" occasionally applies to real fish dish wishes as well.

Whether or not fish are "brain" food, as your mother suggested, it has been shown that making certain fish a regular part of your diet allows you to eat lighter and smarter. A good source of protein, cold water fish also supply us with essential minerals and may well help lower blood cholesterol. Salmon and halibut are good examples of cold water fish.

Ask for suggestions on preparation and preservation of various types of fish at your local deli counter. We're sure you'll get on . . . swimmingly!

ECONOMICALLY
SERVING SEAFOOD

CHINESE SALMON STEAKS

dash	ground ginger	dash
½	garlic clove, finely chopped OR dash of garlic powder	½
2 tbsp.	lime juice	30 mL
2 tsp.	soy sauce	10 mL
½ tsp.	Dijon mustard	2 mL
½ tsp.	vegetable oil	2 mL
½ tsp.	brown sugar	2 mL
dash	cayenne pepper	dash
2 tbsp.	butter	30 mL
2	salmon steaks	2
	toasted sesame seeds	

Heat oven to 425°F (220°C).

Mix the ginger, garlic, lime juice, soy sauce, mustard, oil, brown sugar and cayenne pepper into a magic Oriental sauce.

Use a baking dish large enough to hold the salmon steaks in 1 layer. Grease it with butter. Lay out salmon steaks in the dish. Splash the magic sauce over the fish. Cover the dish with foil and bake in oven for 10 minutes per 1" (2.5 cm) of thickness in your steak. Sprinkle sesame seeds over steaks just before serving.

Serves: 1-2

EPT: 25 minutes

COD AND LEMON SAUTÉ

2 tbsp.	flour	30 mL
¼ tsp.	salt	1 mL
dash	pepper	dash
¼ tsp.	paprika	1 mL
2	cod fillets, 6 oz.(170 g) each	2
2 tbsp.	butter	30 mL
	lemon rind (removed from lemon and thinly sliced)	
	lemon juice (from ½ lemon)	
dash	Tabasco sauce	dash
¼ cup	dry white wine	50 mL

Season flour with salt, pepper and paprika. Dredge (see glossary) cod fillets in flour and set them aside.

In a frying pan, sauté (see glossary again or learn to memorize new terms!) slices of lemon rind in half the butter for 2 minutes.

Pour lemon juice into pan and stir in Tabasco. Throw in cod fillets and fry at high heat until cooked through, turning once. Use the additional butter here if necessary.

Remove cooked fillets to warm platter. Pour the wine into the frying pan and bring to a boil, scraping the sides of the frying pan, and blending the mixture left in the pan with the wine. When the liquid is reduced by half, through evaporation, pour the remainder over the cod and serve immediately.

Serves: 1-2

EPT: 25 minutes

HALIBUT FLORENTINE

2	halibut steaks, 5-7 oz. (140-200 g) each	2
2 tbsp.	flour	30 mL
2 tbsp.	butter	30 mL
	salt and pepper, to taste	
½ lb.	spinach, freshly cooked OR 5 oz. (140 g) frozen (½ pkg.)	250 g
dash	nutmeg	dash
½	garlic clove, finely crushed OR dash of garlic powder	½
1 tbsp.	lemon juice	15 mL

Dust fish with flour (which is a lot easier than trying to dust flour with fish!).

Heat half the butter in a medium hot frying pan and sauté fish for 10 minutes per 1" (2.5 cm) of thickness, turning once halfway through cooking time. Season with salt and pepper.

Boil fresh spinach, in a little water, for 2 minutes or according to package directions if frozen. Drain, then remove the spinach from the pan and dump it on a warm platter. Sprinkle the nutmeg on top of the hot spinach.

Arrange fish on spinach and keep it warm in an oven at low heat.

Toss the remaining butter together with the garlic in a frying pan on medium-high heat. Cook, stirring, until butter starts to turn brown. Stir in lemon juice.

Pour this little bit of heaven over the fish and serve immediately.

Serves: 1-2

EPT: 25 minutes

Uncle Jack Culpepper's Last Word on Women: Men should not worry about not understanding women, most women do not understand themselves.
Aunt Charlotte Culpepper (his wife): I don't understand that last remark!
Uncle Robbie Culpepper (his brother): That's understandable!

HALIBUT STEAKS WITH PECANS

2	halibut steaks, 5-7 oz. (140-200 g) each	2
½ cup	finely chopped pecans	125 mL
2 tbsp.	flour	30 mL
¼ tsp.	salt	1 mL
dash	pepper	dash
1 tbsp.	maple syrup	15 mL
2 tbsp.	vegetable oil	30 mL
	lemon juice, to taste	
	whole pecans for garnish	

Pat halibut dry with a paper towel . . . but don't become too attached!!

Throw the pecans, flour, salt and pepper together on a flat plate.

Using a pastry brush, coat 1 side of each halibut steak with maple syrup, then dredge in the pecan concoction. Now — same approach to the other side of fish.

Heat 1 tbsp. (15 mL) oil in frying pan. Fry halibut at medium heat for 10 minutes per 1" (2.5 cm) of thickness, turning once halfway through cooking time. Use more oil if necessary.

Sprinkle with lemon juice, garnish with whole pecans, then serve.

Serves: 1-2

EPT: 25 minutes

RED SNAPPER LYONNAISE

1 tbsp.	butter	15 mL
2	onions, thinly sliced	2
2 tbsp.	vegetable oil	30 mL
2	red snapper fillets OR steaks, 5-7 oz. (140-200 g) each	2
	salt and pepper, to taste	
¼ cup	grated Parmesan cheese	50 mL
¼ cup	bread crumbs	50 mL

Heat butter in medium hot frying pan. Sauté onions, separated into rings, for 4 minutes (until they go limp) then set them aside.

Brush vegetable oil on both sides of the fish and arrange it on the rack which fits into the broiler pan. Season with salt and pepper.

Stick fish under a preheated medium-high broiler...about 4" (10 cm) from the heat source.

Broil for 10 minutes per 1" (2.5 cm) of thickness. Turn fish once during cooking, 3 minutes before end of cooking time.

Distribute the onions, cheese and bread crumbs on top of the fish, then continue to cook for the final 3 minutes.

Serves: 1-2

EPT: 25 minutes

78

SALMON KANAPASTA

handful	fresh mushrooms, sliced	handful
3 tbsp.	butter, melted	45 mL
1 cup	uncooked macaroni, cooked	250 mL
7.5 oz.	salmon (1 can)	213 g
5 oz.	Cheddar cheese soup	142 mL
2	bread slices, cubed	2

Heat oven to 350°F (180°C).

Sauté mushrooms in 1 tbsp. (15 mL) of butter. Dump cooked macaroni in a greased casserole dish. Sprinkle the mushrooms over macaroni.

Drain salmon (save the juice) and use a fork to flake the salmon over mushrooms. Mix the soup and salmon juice together and pour this succulent seafood sauce over the salmon. Give it a stir. Toss bread cubes into the other 2 tbsp. (30 mL) of melted butter and pour this concoction over salmon as well.

Bake in oven, uncovered, for 20 minutes.

Serves: 1-2

EPT: 35 minutes

SOLE FILLETS WITH DILL

½ tsp.	dill seed	2 mL
dash	celery seed	dash
	salt and pepper, to taste	
2	sole fillets, 4 oz. (115 g) each	2
1 tbsp.	butter	15 mL
½	lemon	½

Toss dill seed, celery seed, salt and pepper together and mix it up. Sprinkle this mixture over 1 side of the fish.

Place the fish, seasoned side up, on a greased broiler pan, then dot with butter. Broil for 10 minutes per inch (2.5 cm) of thickness. Squeeze the ½ lemon over the fish before serving.

Option: You may substitute perch, red snapper or cod for sole.

Serves: 1-2

EPT: 25 minutes

SHRIMP-SMOTHERED SOLE WITH GREEN HOLLANDAISE SAUCE

4	sole fillets, 4 oz. (115 g) each	4
	salt and pepper, to taste	
1	carrot, thinly sliced	1
¼ lb.	cooked baby shrimp	125 g
¼ cup	dry white wine	50 mL
1 cup	water	250 mL
¼ tsp.	crushed tarragon	1 mL

Heat oven to 450°F (230°C).

Season both sides of sole with salt and pepper. Then roll fillets, starting at narrow end.

Dump carrot slices in a shallow ovenproof dish. Pile the sole rolls on top. Throw most of the shrimp over rolls, saving a few for garnish. Taste the wine. One more sip. Now say the name of this recipe 10 times quickly. (Nice try!) O.K., that's enough . . . now pour wine over the poor fish and shrimp. Add the water. Sprinkle tarragon over the entire delicacy.

Cover the dish with foil and bake in oven for 15 minutes. Drain off liquid. Top the fish with Green Hollandaise Sauce (see following recipe) and garnish with the shrimp you saved just for this purpose.

Serves: 1-2

EPT: 35 minutes

GREEN HOLLANDAISE SAUCE

½ tbsp.	lemon juice	7 mL
½ tbsp.	white wine	7 mL
2	egg yolks*	2
½ cup	warm melted butter	125 mL
1 tbsp.	chopped parsley	15 mL
1 tbsp.	finely chopped green onion	15 mL

Toss the lemon juice, wine and egg yolks into a blender. Blend on high for 15 seconds. Then, while blender motor is running at medium speed, very slowly and steadily add warm melted butter. (If butter is too hot, Hollandaise Sauce will separate. We want a nice thick sauce.)

Cover the blender and set it on high speed for 1 minute. Dump the parsley and green onion in the blender and blend for 1 more minute.

Yield: approximately ½ cup (125 mL) of sauce

EPT: 10 minutes

* Here are 4 methods of separating yolks and whites:

1. Buy a separator at the store (white runs through little hole while yolk stays in cup).
2. Crack egg carefully and by juggling between the 2 half shells, separate yolk from white.
3. Crack egg and empty into the palm of your hand. The white will run through your fingers and the yolk stays. Stand over the sink, please!
4. Crack the egg into a bowl and carefully lift the yolk out.

STUFFED TROUT

2	medium, whole trout	2
	salt, to taste	
2	bacon strips	2
2 tbsp.	vegetable oil	30 mL

Stuffing Ingredients:

¾ cup	cooked rice	175 mL
3 tbsp.	diced onion	45 mL
1	tomato, diced	1
1 tsp.	salt	5 mL
dash	garlic salt	dash
	pepper, to taste	

Using a sharp knife, slit the trout open between the head and tail. Remove bones and guts. (Or buy them cleaned, you wimp!) Then rub the insides with salt. Set them aside.

Combine all the stuffing ingredients in a bowl. Mix well.

Heat the broiler to 500°F (260°C).

Stuff each trout with the stuffing mix. Take a strip of bacon and wrap it around the trout . . . securing with wooden toothpicks. Brush the outside of the fish with the vegetable oil.

Broil until done (about 15 minutes) and turn the trout over once about halfway through the cooking time.

Serves: 1-2

EPT: 25 minutes

BBQ BONANZA

BBQ BONANZA

BBQ NOTES

Gentlemen, here is another one of those prehistoric preoccupations which have built-in benefits for impressing the cavewoman of your dreams. Sure, you have to build a fire outside . . . but building a fire outside to heat the meal can build a fire inside to seal the deal. And guess what?? It may look like a lot of time and trouble taken on her behalf . . . but, in fact, there are no zillion dishes, pots and pans to do afterwards. And, if you really want to rack up a couple quadrillion points . . . try a winter BBQ! It's as easy, really, as the summertime version . . . but the seasonal shift makes it a special event. Scoot out occasionally to check the meal in your big fur coat, serve it with a smile, and I guarantee she'll tickle your aurora borealis.

Notes on the . . .

Flavor Whether your barbecuing takes place in a large or small charcoal pit in the backyard, inside the roasting oven of your kitchen, or out on the balcony, deck or patio with a gas or charcoal barbecue grill, the one distinctive aspect of the barbecue experience is the flavor.

The unique flavor of barbecued meats comes from the singeing of the meat's surface and from the smoke that rises from the smoldering meat drippings.

In addition to the natural flavor of the meats, there are also flavor "enhancers". They are often a "wood-smoke" style in the form of wood chips. The various types include oak, hickory, alder, apple, orange, cherry and other "flavors".

When using wood-flavoring chips, toss a few chips on the coals just before the meat is removed from the barbecue grill.

See the list of marinades for another way to influence the flavor and texture of your barbecue specialties.

Propane Propane barbecues are inexpensive to operate and allow temperature control as well as relief from the messy and dangerous job of starting a charcoal fire.

The propane barbecue is easy to turn on and off and the even distribution of heat makes it a better choice for roasting foods.

While the initial price may be much higher than a charcoal barbecue, the long-term savings are greater. The cost of bags of charcoal and fire-starting paraphenalia mount up quickly if you are a barbecue addict.

Charcoal Charcoal is purchased in either lump or briquet form. Briquets burn without sparking, produce uniform heat and hold that heat a long time.

Lump charcoal is less expensive and burns with a more authentic wood aroma.

Most beginners use far more charcoal than necessary. Make the single layer of charcoal a little wider all round than the area of the food to be cooked. A handful of charcoal is enough for small barbecue jobs like hamburgers and hot dogs.

BBQ NOTES (cont'd.)

Fire   Briquets burn from the bottom to the top, so they require draft from below. Some barbecue grills have an open mesh grate to create this draft. In other grills, you may need to prepare the firebed for an effective fire. If the bottom of the grill is solid, cover it with a layer of sand or gravel. This helps the air to circulate.

Charcoal is a stubborn fuel, but there are several ways to coax the fire:

1. Use small pieces of cardboard as kindling.
2. Use an electric starter. Just place the hot coil on the bottom of the briquets and they begin to heat quickly.
3. Use pressed petroleum product chips. Sprinkle small pieces around the charcoal and light each individually.
4. Use a liquid starter. While liquid starters are simple and effective, great care must be taken whenever they are used. Pour approximately ½ cup (125 mL) of the starter fluid on a pyramid-shaped pile of briquets. Wait a few minutes to allow the fluid to soak into the coals, then throw a lighted match onto the charcoal.

Always keep a fire extinguisher or container of sand or salt nearby, in case the fire gets out of control. Water may not extinguish the fire and, in fact, may splash or spread burning starter fluid onto some other flammable object.

The beginner barbecue chef often tries to cook over open flames rather than wait for the coals to turn themselves into little furnaces. Allow the coals to burn to a grey color to get the even, constant heat needed for successful barbecuing. This also allows the toxic fumes from the burning charcoal and starter fluid to be burnt off before putting your food over the fire.

Temperature   A grill thermometer is the best way to tell when the fire is at cooking temperature. Another way is to hold your hand at the meat-cooking level and count seconds until the heat forces you to remove your hand.

As a general rule, if you can only hold your hand over the heat for 2-3 seconds, the fire is ready.

For you technical types, the recommended temperature is between 300-350°F (150-180°C).

If you want low heat (or "slow fire", as BBQ professionals call it), use tongs to spread the coals in a checkerboard pattern over the firebed.

Hand Jive   One way to test the progress of the meat being prepared for your guests is to use the palm of your hand as a guide. Take a look at the palm of your left hand. Use your right thumb and press it against the soft edge of your palm just below the little finger. When cooked meat feels this tender, it is rare. Now press that hefty piece of muscle and fat just below your left thumb. When cooked meat feels this consistent, it is medium. Now press the flesh in the center of the palm of your hand. When cooked meat feels this tough, it is well-done (P.S.: Take your oven mitt off first!).

Food

Barbecue Marinades   As previously mentioned, one approach to food preparation is to "marinate" or soak the meat, fish or poultry in a mixture designed to soften the meat, bring out some flavor, add some new flavor, or all of the above.

85

BEEF MARINADE

1 cup	olive oil	250 mL
½ cup	red wine	125 mL
2	garlic cloves, finely diced	2
1	onion, finely chopped	1
2 tsp.	salt	30 mL
¼ tsp.	pepper	1 mL
½ tsp.	oregano	2 mL
½ tsp.	sweet basil	2 mL

Combine the above ingredients in a loaf pan or small casserole dish. Make enough marinade to submerge the meat and put the entire operation in the refrigerator. For best results, marinate overnight or earlier the same day.

Yield: 1½ cups (375 mL)

LAMB MARINADE

1 cup	vegetable oil	250 mL
1 cup	red wine	250 mL
6	garlic cloves, finely diced	6
2 tsp.	salt	10 mL
¼ tsp.	pepper	1 mL
1 tbsp.	chopped mint leaves	15 mL
	rosemary (just a touch)	

Combine the above ingredients and follow the same procedure as Beef Marinade.

Yield: 2 cups (500 mL)

PORK MARINADE

1 cup	olive oil	250 mL
½ cup	dry white wine	125 mL
1 tbsp.	vinegar	15 mL
1	onion, finely chopped	1
2	garlic cloves, finely diced	2
½ tsp.	caraway seed	2 mL

Combine the above ingredients and follow same procedure as Beef Marinade.

Yield: 1½ cups (375 mL)

POULTRY MARINADE

1 cup	vegetable oil	250 mL
½ cup	dry white wine	125 mL
1 tsp.	vinegar	5 mL
1	garlic clove, finely diced	1
½ tsp.	paprika	2 mL
¼ tsp.	tarragon	1 mL
2 tsp.	salt	10 mL

Combine the above ingredients and follow same procedure as Beef Marinade.

Yield: 1½ cups (375 mL)

FISH MARINADE

½ cup	vegetable oil	125 mL
½ cup	dry white wine	125 mL
2	garlic cloves, finely diced	2
¼ tsp.	pepper	1 mL
1 tsp.	Worcestershire sauce	5 mL
1 tsp.	paprika	5 mL
1 tsp.	salt	5 mL

Combine the ingredients and follow same procedure as Beef Marinade.

Yield: 1 cup (250 mL)

87

HICKORY BBQ SAUCE

| 1 cup | regular BBQ sauce | 250 mL |
| 1 tbsp. | liquid hickory smoke flavoring | 15 mL |

Combine ingredients and spread over your BBQ masterpiece.

Yield: 1 cup (250 mL)

HONEY AND GARLIC BBQ SAUCE

| 1 cup | honey | 250 mL |
| 1 tsp. | garlic powder | 5 mL |

Combine ingredients and heat in saucepan. Blend well and let simmer for 5 minutes. Spread on finished cooked meats. Great for pork ribs and roasts.

Yield: 1 cup (250 mL)

PINEAPPLE BBQ SAUCE

| 1 cup | crushed pineapple from a can, drained | 250 mL |
| ½ cup | regular BBQ sauce | 125 mL |

Combine these ingredients and spread on chicken and pork delights.

Yield: 1½ cups (375 mL)

SWEET & SOUR BBQ SAUCE

¼ cup	cornstarch	50 mL
½ cup	cold water	125 mL
1 cup	water	250 mL
⅔ cup	sugar	150 mL
⅓ cup	vinegar	75 mL
⅔ cup	regular BBQ sauce	150 mL

Combine cornstarch and cold water to make a paste.

Mix the rest of the ingredients in another pan and heat on the stove at medium high heat.

When this mixture boils, gradually add the cornstarch mixture until it is at your desired thickness.

Let cool and use as BBQ sauce.

Yield: 3 cups (750 mL)

BBQ HAMBURGERS

3	bread slices	3
½ cup	milk	125 mL
1 lb.	ground beef	500 g
½	onion, chopped	½
1	egg	1
½ cup	chopped bacon	125 mL
¼ tsp.	garlic salt	1 mL
	salt and pepper, to taste	
	BBQ sauce	

Tear crusts off bread.

Soak bread in milk, then mix all ingredients together in the same bowl. Shape the mixture into patties. Grill on medium fire and brush with BBQ sauce, your own recipe or your favorite commercial variety, before serving.

Serves: 2-4

EPT: 30 minutes

BBQ MEAT LOAF

4	bread slices	4
½ cup	milk	125 mL
1 lb.	ground beef	500 g
½ lb.	ground pork	250 g
2	eggs	2
1	onion, chopped	1
½ tsp.	garlic salt	2 mL
1 tsp.	Worcestershire sauce	5 mL
¼ cup	ketchup	50 mL
	salt and pepper, to taste	
	BBQ sauce	

Tear crusts off bread.

Soak bread in milk and then combine all ingredients in the same bowl. Mix and pack firmly and then shape the entire mixture into a loaf.

Wrap the loaf tightly in foil and cook over a medium fire for 1½ hours.

Remove the foil and cook for 20 minutes, brushing with BBQ sauce.

Serves: 2-4

EPT: 2 hours

89

BBQ CHUCK OR ROUND STEAK

For best results, buy a steak 1-1½" (2.5-4 cm) thick.

Marinate steak for 1 day in the Beef Marinade, page 86.

Cook over slow fire for 30 minutes or to personal taste. Aromatic wood chips may be used.

Brush with homemade or store bought BBQ sauce before serving.

Serves: 1 steak for 1-2, depending on size.

EPT: 30 minutes

BBQ PORTERHOUSE, T-BONE, CLUB, RIB, SIRLOIN STEAK

For best results, buy a steak 1" (2.5 cm) thick.

Marinate for 1 hour in Beef Marinade, page 86, and then cook until done to your personal taste. See Barbecue Notes on flavor, page 84.

Aromatic wood chips may be used.

Brush with your choice of BBQ sauce before serving.

Serves: 1 steak for 1-2, depending on size.

EPT: 20 minutes

BBQ PRIME RIB

Season the meat by rubbing with salt, pepper, garlic salt and thyme.

Place the meat on a spit so that the weight is evenly distributed.

Cook over a medium fire for 30 minutes per pound (500 g) of meat. (More or less meat requires more or less time over the fire.) Aromatic wood chips may be used.

Brush with BBQ sauce before serving.

Serving: ¾ lb. (350 g) per person

EPT: 30 minutes per pound

Uncle Robbie "Red" Culpepper's Hot Tips for BBQ Maniacs: To get the perfect steak, first sear both sides over medium heat to capture flavor and natural juices. Cook on one side until the blood rises to the top of the steak, then turn the steak and cook for several minutes while adding BBQ sauce. Use "Hand Jive", page 85, to check readiness — then exercise your rights as a carnivore. Remember, steak cooks more thoroughly over medium rather than high heat.

BBQ LAMB CHOPS

Buy precut lamb chops or cut between the bones on a lamb rack. Marinate in Lamb Marinade, page 86, for 3 hours. Cook over medium coals for 25-30 minutes. Brush with mint sauce before serving.

Serve: 3-4 chops per person.

EPT: 35 minutes

LAMB EN BROCHETTE

Cut 2 lbs. (1 kg) lean lamb meat into 1" (2.5 cm) chunks and marinate in Lamb Marinade, page 86, for 1 hour. Thread onto skewers and BBQ for 20 minutes. Brush with mint sauce before serving.

For additional flavor, add chunks of onion and green pepper on your skewer, between the pieces of lamb.

Serves: 2-4

EPT: 25 minutes

BBQ HAM STEAK

Grill ham steaks over a medium fire then brush with honey before serving. You can get them from your butcher as thick as you like. I would suggest that you get them cut about ½" (1.5 cm) thick.

EPT: 10 minutes

BBQ PORK BUTT

Marinate the pork in Pork Marinade, page 86, for 1 day (24 hours). Place pork butt on a spit and roast over a slow fire for approximately 3 hours. Rotate slightly every 15 minutes unless you have an automatic rotisserie. Hickory smoke chips may be used. Be sure the pork is cooked all the way through. Brush with BBQ sauce before serving.

Serves: 1 person per pound (500 g) of pork purchased.

EPT: 3 hours

BBQ STUFFED PORK LOIN

Take a knife or skewer and run it right through one end of the pork loin and out the other end. In this "tunnel" or opening through the center of the pork loin, stuff pork sausage, or apple slices, or pitted prunes. Marinate in Pork Marinade, page 86, for 1 day (24 hours).

Place the meat on a spit and cook over a low heat for about 1½ hours. Brush with BBQ sauce before serving.

Be sure the loin is thoroughly cooked.

Serves: 1 person per pound (500 g) of pork purchased.

EPT: 2 hours

BBQ PORK SPARE RIBS

Marinate ribs in Pork Marinade, page 86, for 1 day (24 hours). BBQ over low heat (200-225°F [100-110°C]), brushing regularly with BBQ sauce, for 2 hours.

Be sure the ribs are cooked all the way through.

EPT: 2 hours

"Chicken Charlie" Culpepper's Poultry Pickin' Hints: When you have guests coming over for a BBQ experience, allow approximately 1 pound (500 g) of poultry per person. So, if you're expecting 8 people at your BBQ Bash, buy an 8-lb. (3.5 kg) chicken or turkey and have enough for everyone . . . or buy 2, 4-lb. (2 kg) chickens to be BBQ'd at the same time and cut your cooking time in half. You can certainly buy bigger for those hearty appetites . . . but the "pound of poultry per person" rule will keep you and your guests satisfied.

BBQ WHOLE CHICKEN

Remove chicken parts such as neck, gizzard, liver, etc. Then rinse inside and outside of chicken with cold water. Place chicken on a spit, brush inside and outside with Poultry Marinade, page 87, and roast over medium fire for 25-30 minutes per lb. (500 g). For example — a 3 lb. (1.5 kg) chicken (for serving 3 people) requires about 1½ hours roasting.

Serves: 1 person per pound (500 g)

EPT: 25-30 minutes per pound

BBQ CHICKEN BREASTS

Marinate chicken breasts in Poultry Marinade, page 87, for 1 hour. Drain off excess marinade and cook the chicken over a medium heat. Brush with BBQ sauce before serving.

EPT: 25-30 minutes per pound

SKEWERED CHICKEN LIVERS

18	chicken livers	18
	salt and pepper, to taste	
6	bacon slices	6
18	mushrooms	18
1 tbsp.	vegetable oil	15 mL
½ cup	bread crumbs	125 mL
¼ cup	butter OR margarine	50 mL

Rinse chicken livers in cold water and pat dry. Season with salt and pepper. Cut bacon slices into 3 pieces.

Put on each skewer: One cut piece of bacon, a mushroom and a chicken liver, and keep alternating until the skewer is fully loaded. Roll the loaded skewer in the oil (or brush with oil). Sprinkle bread crumbs over each loaded skewer and grill over medium coals.

Brush with melted butter or margarine before serving.

Serves: 2-3

EPT: 20 minutes

BBQ WHOLE TURKEY

Brush whole turkey with Poultry Marinade (page 87). Wrestle it onto a spit and roast over medium fire for 35-40 minutes per lb. (500 g). For example, a 10 lb. (4.5 kg) turkey will need approximately 6 hours roasting. Now is a good time to read that novel! Aromatic wood chips may be used. You can check the weight on the package or at the store!

Serves: 1 person per pound (500 g)

EPT: 35-40 minutes per pound

93

BBQ Preparation ... Oysters, Scallops, Lobster, Shrimp, Halibut and Salmon Chunks

Wrap each bite-size chunk of the above in bacon. Secure each wrapped piece on a skewer. Cook over high heat (near the center of the fire) until all sides are brown. Then finish cooking over a slow fire (nearer the edge of the fire) for 3-5 minutes or until the seafood is cooked.

EPT: 10 minutes

BACON BBQ'D TROUT

2	eggs	2
1 tbsp.	milk	15 mL
½ tsp.	allspice	2 mL
½ tsp.	garlic salt	2 mL
1	trout (per person)	1
1-2	bacon slices (per trout)	1-2
1	lemon, sliced	1

Blend all ingredients, except the trout, bacon and lemon, together.

Coat the trout inside and out with the mixture and stuff with lemon slices.

Wrap each trout in 1 or 2 strips of bacon (make them secure with toothpicks) and place on greased grill, or in a greased wire basket, or foil.

Cook over medium coals, turning once, for 20 minutes or until fish flakes. Serve with lemon wedges.

EPT: 30 minutes

SALMON STEAKS

Brush ¾" (2 cm) thick salmon steaks with Fish Marinade, page 87, or BBQ sauce and cook over medium fire for 15 minutes. Turn once about halfway through cooking time.

Serve: 6 - 8 oz. steak per person

EPT: 15 minutes

SCALLOP AND SHRIMP KEBABS

¼ tsp.	marjoram	1 mL
¼ lb.	butter, melted	125 g
16	scallops, rinsed	16
16	shrimps, cleaned	16
	salt and pepper, to taste	
8	bacon slices	8
1 tbsp.	lemon juice	15 mL

Mix the marjoram into the melted butter. Dip scallops and shrimps into this melted butter mixture. Season each with salt and pepper.

Arrange 2 scallops and 2 shrimps on a skewer with 2 slices of bacon. Weave bacon between shellfish.

BBQ over charcoal. When finished cooking, sprinkle melted butter and lemon juice over each skewer and serve.

Serves: 2-3

EPT: 25 minutes

BBQ BREAD

1	French bread loaf	1
½ cup	butter OR margarine	125 mL
1 tbsp.	prepared mustard	15 mL
½ cup	grated Parmesan cheese	125 mL
¼ cup	chopped parsley	50 mL

Slice bread in 1" (2.5 cm) slices, cutting down to (but not through) the bottom crust.

Combine all other ingredients in a bowl. Mix well and spread generously on both sides of each slice of bread. Wrap the loaf tightly in foil.

Place near the edge of the grill (or in the kitchen oven at 350°F [180°C]) for 30 minutes.

Serves: 2-4

EPT: 40 minutes

BBQ CELERY BREAD

1	French bread loaf	1
½ cup	butter OR margarine	125 mL
½ tsp.	celery seed	2 mL
¼ tsp.	paprika	1 mL
dash	cayenne pepper	dash
¼ tsp.	salt	1 mL

Slice all the crust from the bread. Cut the loaf lengthwise . . . almost through to the bottom and then slice (the way you would any normal loaf of bread) at 2" (5 cm) intervals . . . still not cutting all the way through to the bottom.

Blend the butter or margarine with all the remaining ingredients. Spread this mixture over all surfaces of the loaf (except the bottom). Wrap tightly in foil and place over high heat (or bake in the kitchen oven at 450°F [230°C]) for 5 minutes.

Serves: 2-4

EPT: 10 minutes

BBQ POTATOES LYONNAISE

4	potatoes, peeled and thinly sliced	4
2	medium onions, thinly sliced	2
¼ cup	margarine	50 mL
	salt and pepper, to taste	

Mix all ingredients thoroughly in a bowl and then wrap them tightly in separate portions with foil and BBQ over medium-high heat for 30-45 minutes . . . turning once about halfway through the cooking time.

Serves: 2-4.

EPT: 55 minutes

BBQ TEXAS CORN

4 ears	corn, husks removed	4 ears
¼ cup	butter OR margarine, melted	50 mL
1 tsp.	chili powder	5 mL
¼ tsp.	paprika	1 mL

Blend the butter or margarine and spices in a bowl and rub this mixture over each ear of corn.

Wrap corn tightly in foil and cook over medium-high heat for 30 minutes . . . turning the package over once about halfway through cooking time.

Serves: 2-4

EPT: 40 minutes

Uncle Yardley Culpepper calls barbecuing: "North America's Favorite Outdoor Activity". Friends, fresh air, fun and food make a lovely combination in every season. Today's hibachi and high-rise crowd make it possible for us to have BBQ dates any day or night of the year.

QUIET DINNERS FOR TWO

QUIET DINNERS FOR TWO

WARNING! The following recipes are for adults only!! The author and publisher assume no responsibility for actions before, during or after these bodacious banquet bouquets are served.

Menu #1

Tomato Onion Salad
Oven-Baked Salmon Steaks
Lemon Chive Potatoes
Green Beans Almondine
Peaches 'n' Custard

Wine — Chardonnay

EPT: 60 minutes

TOMATO ONION SALAD

3	tomatoes	3
¼	head lettuce	¼
½	onion, finely diced	½
1 tbsp.	red wine vinegar	15 mL
1 tbsp.	salad oil	15 mL

Take a pot big enough for the 3 tomatoes, fill it with water and bring to a boil. Cut an 'X' on the smooth (bottom) end of the tomatoes. Add tomatoes to boiling water for 30 seconds. Then remove tomatoes and immediately stick them under cold water. Peel them.

Shred the lettuce and place evenly on salad plates. Slice peeled tomatoes and dump them on the lettuce. Sprinkle the diced onion on top of the tomato slices.

Sprinkle each Tomato Onion Salad with vinegar and oil.

Serves: 2

OVEN-BAKED SALMON STEAKS

2 tbsp.	butter OR margarine	30 mL
½ tsp.	salt	2 mL
¼ tsp.	pepper	1 mL
2	salmon steaks, 6-8 oz. (170-250 g) each	2
¼ cup	flour	50 mL
½ tsp.	paprika	2 mL
2	lemon wedges	2
1	tomato, cut into wedges	1

Heat oven to 500°F (260°C). Melt butter in a shallow baking dish in the oven. Sprinkle salt and pepper over the salmon steaks. Coat them with flour and slide them into the baking dish. Sprinkle paprika over fish.

Bake, uncovered, for 10-15 minutes, until the fish flakes easily with a fork. Garnish with lemon and tomato wedges before serving.

Serves: 2

LEMON CHIVE POTATOES

2	medium potatoes	2
1 tbsp.	butter OR margarine	15 mL
1 tsp.	lemon juice	5 mL
2 tbsp.	chopped chives OR green onions	30 mL

Peel potatoes and cut them in half. Boil until tender (approximately 15-20 minutes).

When potatoes are almost cooked, heat oven to 500°F (260°C).

Throw potatoes into an ungreased 1-quart (1 L) casserole dish. Heave into the oven, uncovered, and bake for 15 minutes.

Add remaining ingredients. Slosh potatoes around in them until well coated, then serve.

Serves: 2

GREEN BEANS ALMONDINE

½ lb.	green beans, fresh OR frozen	250 g
2 tbsp.	butter	30 mL
1 tbsp.	sliced almonds	15 mL
dash	salt	dash
dash	pepper	dash
dash	garlic powder	dash

If fresh, boil beans in a little water until tender (5-8 minutes). If frozen, follow directions on the package.

Melt butter in frying pan at medium-high heat. Dump in the almonds, salt, pepper and garlic and fry until almonds are golden. Now add the drained beans, stir-fry until thoroughly mixed and heated. Serve.

Serves: 2

PEACHES 'N' CUSTARD

½ cup	vanilla pudding, canned OR from mix	125 mL
14 oz.	can sliced peaches, drained	398 mL
2 tsp.	raspberry jelly	10 mL

Mix pudding and then put in refrigerator to chill.

When ready to serve dessert, divide the peaches between 2 dessert plates.

Spoon pudding over peaches and top each serving with 1 tsp. (5 mL) jelly.

Serves: 2

Tossed Salad with Oil and Vinegar Dressing
Stuffed Pork Chops
Buttered Broccoli
Roast Potatoes
Chocolate Peanut Parfait

Wine — Riesling

EPT: 60 minutes

TOSSED SALAD WITH OIL AND VINEGAR DRESSING

½	head lettuce	½
2	radishes, sliced	2
½	green pepper, diced	½
2	tomatoes, cut into wedges	2

Break lettuce into bite-sized pieces and then dump it, along with the radishes, green pepper and tomatoes, into a salad bowl. Just before serving, slosh the Oil and Vinegar Dressing (recipe below) over the tossed salad.

Oil and Vinegar Dressing

2 tbsp.	salad oil	30 mL
1 tbsp.	vinegar	15 mL
¼ tsp.	salt	1 mL
1	garlic clove, finely chopped OR dash of garlic powder	1
dash	pepper	dash

Fling these ingredients into a tightly covered container. Give it a good shake before dumping over tossed salad.

Serves: 2

STUFFED PORK CHOPS

2	boneless pork chops, 1" (2.5 cm) thick	2
2	ham slices	2
2	Swiss cheese slices	2
⅓ cup	flour	75 mL
2	eggs, beaten	2
½ cup	bread crumbs	125 mL
1 tbsp.	vegetable oil	15 mL

Slit each pork chop horizontally to form a pocket (or have the butcher at the supermarket do it for you!). Squish a slice of ham and a slice of cheese into each newly created pocket. Secure with toothpicks or string.

Dip each chop into flour. Shake off excess. Dip chops into egg, then dip into crumbs.

Heat oil in a casserole dish in the oven at 350°F (180°C). Toss the chops into the dish and cover. Bake for 30 minutes.

Serves: 2

102

BUTTERED BROCCOLI

1 lb.	broccoli	500 g
3 cups	water	750 mL
¼ tsp.	salt	1 mL
1 tbsp.	butter	15 mL
dash	pepper	dash

Trim the leaves off the broccoli and remove the tough ends of the lower stalks. Break the broccoli into pieces. Boil the water and salt. Throw the broccoli in and cook at a boil for 2-3 minutes, until tender.

Remove broccoli and heap the butter over it before serving.

Serves: 2

ROAST POTATOES

2	large potatoes	2
½ tsp.	salt	2 mL
3 cups	water	750 mL
2 tbsp.	butter	30 mL
	salt and pepper, to taste	
½ tsp.	paprika	2 mL

Peel the potatoes and cut in half. Dump potatoes into salted water and bring to a boil. Let cook for about 15 minutes.

Remove potatoes from pot, while they are still a little firm, and throw them onto a baking sheet. Baste with butter and season with salt, pepper and paprika.

Bake in oven at 400°F (200°C) until the potatoes are golden brown, about 20 minutes.

Serves: 2

CHOCOLATE PEANUT PARFAIT

2 cups	chocolate pudding, canned or from mix	500 mL
½ cup	whipping cream, whipped	125 mL
3 tbsp.	chopped peanuts	45 mL
2	maraschino cherries	2

Take 2 parfait glasses and plop ½ cup (125 mL) of pudding into each. Top with ¼ cup (50 mL) whipped cream and 1 tbsp. (15 mL) peanuts.

Now add the other ½ cup (125 mL) of pudding to each glass. Top with remaining whipped cream and garnish with peanuts and a maraschino cherry.

Serves: 2

103

Menu #3

Lettuce Wedges with Roquefort Dressing
Chicken Apricot
Buttered Green Beans
Baked Potatoes
Crème de Menthe Parfait

Wine — Sauvignon Blanc OR Chardonnay

EPT: 60 minutes

LETTUCE WEDGES WITH ROQUEFORT DRESSING

½ cup	sour cream	125 mL
¼ cup	crumbled blue cheese	50 mL
½ tsp.	lemon juice	2 mL
¼ tsp.	salt	1 mL
½	head lettuce, cut in wedges	½

Fling the sour cream, blue cheese, lemon and salt together. Cover and refrigerate for at least 1 hour. (The longer it sits, the richer the flavor.)

Dump lettuce wedges onto salad plates and plop the dressing on top just before serving.

Serves: 2

CHICKEN APRICOT

2	chicken breasts	2
	salt and pepper, to taste	
1	small can apricot halves	1
¼ cup	water	50 mL
1 tbsp.	sugar	15 mL
dash	cinnamon	dash
3 tbsp.	cornstarch	45 mL
⅓ cup	cold water	75 mL

Heat oven to 350°F (180°c).

Hack each chicken breast lengthwise into 2 pieces. Toss them onto a baking sheet. Season with salt and pepper. Bake in oven for approximately 20 minutes, until chicken is golden.

While the chicken bakes, make the sauce. Drain the apricots (save the juice). Throw the ¼ cup (50 mL) water and the apricot juice into a pot. Add the sugar and a dash of cinnamon. Bring to a boil.

Mix the cornstarch with the ⅓ cup (75 mL) of cold water. Gradually add this mixture to the boiling concoction, stirring constantly. Turn down the heat. Heave in the apricot halves and simmer for 5 minutes. Pour this sauce over the baked chicken just before serving.

Serves: 2

BUTTERED GREEN BEANS

½ lb.	green beans, fresh OR frozen	250 g
1 tbsp.	butter	15 mL
dash	salt	dash
dash	pepper	dash

Toss green beans into a pot of boiling water and boil until tender (7-10 minutes). Drain beans. Just before serving, plop the butter on top and add a dash of salt and pepper.

Serves: 2

BAKED POTATOES

2	medium potatoes	2
1 tbsp.	vegetable oil	15 mL
	bacon bits, chopped chives, sour cream as garnish	

Heat oven to 400°F (200°C). Wash and then rub the potatoes with vegetable oil. Wrap each potato in aluminum foil (or, if you like a crispy skin on your potatoes, omit the aluminum foil). Prick the wrapped potatoes with a fork to allow steam to escape while baking. Bake for about 1 hour, until potatoes are tender.

To serve, cut potatoes in half lengthwise about ¾ of the way through. Press potato ends and the potato will open up. Serve with small dishes of bacon bits, chives and sour cream on the side.

Serves: 2

CRÈME DE MENTHE PARFAIT

2 oz.	vanilla ice cream	60 mL
2 oz.	crème de menthe	60 mL
¼ cup	whipping cream, whipped	50 mL
2	maraschino cherries	2

Half fill 2 parfait glasses with ice cream. Pour 1 oz. (30 mL) of crème de menthe into each glass. Dump another layer of ice cream on top. Knead, push, pull and pummel the ice cream just a tad . . . so that the liqueur spreads. Top with whipped cream and a maraschino cherry.

Keep in the freezer until ready to serve.

Serves: 2

Aunt Clara Culpepper's Advice to the Lovelorn: If you put two men in the same room, one with a toothache and the other in love, the man with the toothache will go to sleep first.

Tomato Grapefruit Salad
Chicken Supreme
Parsley Boiled Potatoes
Buttered Brussels Sprouts
Apricot Flambé

Wine — Sauvignon Blanc

EPT: 60 minutes

TOMATO GRAPEFRUIT SALAD

¼	head romaine lettuce	¼
8 oz.	can grapefruit sections, drained	250 mL
1	tomato, cut in wedges	1
1	green pepper, cut in thin strips	1
	sweet 'n' sour salad dressing, to taste	

Arrange lettuce on 2 salad plates. Dump grapefruit and tomato wedges on top followed by the green pepper strips.

Dribble the dressing over each salad and serve.

Serves: 2

CHICKEN SUPREME

2	boneless chicken breasts	2
dash	salt	dash
10 oz.	cream of mushroom soup (straight from the can)	284 mL
½ cup	water	125 mL
handful	mushrooms, sliced	handful
2 tbsp.	sherry	30 mL
1 tbsp.	chopped parsley	15 mL

Chuck chicken breasts into a small pot and barely cover with water. Add a dash of salt. Then simmer for 15 minutes. DO NOT BOIL.

Meanwhile, in another pot, cook the mushroom soup and water for 5 minutes. Flip the mushrooms and sherry into this concoction and simmer for an additional 5 minutes.

Cut each of the poached chicken breasts into 3-4 pieces. Lay the chicken on a serving plate and slop the mushroom supreme sauce over the top.

Sprinkle parsley over the dish just before serving.

Serves: 2

PARSLEY BOILED POTATOES

6-8	small potatoes	6-8
2 tbsp.	butter	30 mL
2 tbsp.	chopped parsley	30 mL

Scrub the unpeeled potatoes with a brush. Stick them in a pot. Barely cover with salted water and bring to a boil. Turn the heat down to medium-low and cook until tender (about 25 minutes).

Drain potatoes, plop butter on top and sprinkle with parsley. Stir around in the pot and then place potatoes on a serving dish.

Serves: 2

BUTTERED BRUSSELS SPROUTS

10 oz.	Brussels sprouts, fresh OR frozen	284 g
2 tbsp.	butter	30 mL
¼	onion, diced	¼
4	bacon strips, diced	4
	salt and pepper, to taste	

Cook fresh Brussels sprouts in just enough boiling water to cover them, until tender (about 10 minutes). If frozen, cook according to package instructions. Do not overcook.

While sprouts cook, melt butter and fry the onion and bacon on medium-high until crisp.

Pop the cooked Brussels sprouts into the onion/bacon mixture and add a dash of salt and pepper. Continue to fry for another 3-5 minutes.

Serves: 2

APRICOT FLAMBÉ

2	large scoops vanilla ice cream	2
2 tbsp.	strawberry jam	30 mL
2 tbsp.	sugar	30 mL
1 cup	canned apricot halves, drained (save the juice)	250 mL
½ tsp.	lemon juice	2 mL
2 tsp.	brandy	10 mL
1	fire extinguisher (keep it handy!)	1

Scoop ice cream into 2 large balls and place in freezer while preparing sauce.

Dump jam, sugar, apricot juice and lemon juice into a small saucepan over medium heat. Cook, stirring occasionally, until syrupy (about 5 minutes). Add apricot halves and heat through. Try to avoid touching or tasting the syrup with tongue or fingers — it is very, very hot!

Douse the apricot halves with the brandy and ignite immediately. Spoon (with a big long-handled spoon) the still-flaming apricots and sauce from the pot onto ice cream and serve.

Serves: 2

107

Spinach Salad
Veal Piccata
Zucchini Parmesan
Au Gratin Potatoes
Chocolate Mocha Dessert

Wine — Italian White OR Riesling

EPT: 60 minutes

SPINACH SALAD

½ lb.	spinach leaves	250 g
1	small onion, sliced	1
3	radishes, sliced	3
2	eggs, boiled and chopped	2
1 tbsp.	bacon bits	15 mL
½ cup	Oil and Vinegar Dressing, page 102	125 mL

Tear spinach into bite-size pieces and separate onion slices into rings. Toss spinach, onion rings, radishes, eggs and bacon bits in and around a bowl. Serve the salad with the dressing on the side.

Serves: 2

VEAL PICCATA

2	veal cutlets	2
⅓ cup	flour	75 mL
1	egg	1
⅓ cup	bread crumbs	75 mL
	salt and pepper, to taste	
	uncooked spaghetti, enough for 2	
handful	mushrooms, sliced	handful
½	onion, diced	½
2	ham slices, cut into strips	2
7½ oz.	can tomato sauce	213 mL
¼ cup	grated Parmesan cheese	50 mL

Pound the cutlets thin. Dip cutlets in flour, then in egg and, finally, in bread crumbs. Then fry cutlets, seasoned with salt and pepper, until golden brown.

Cook spaghetti according to the package instructions. Dump mushrooms, onions and ham in a frying pan and sauté until onions are soft and golden and mushrooms are brownish. Throw tomato sauce in with this mixture, stir and simmer for 10 minutes. (For extra seasoning, you may add ¼ tsp (1 mL) of garlic powder, oregano and/or Italian seasoning to this mixture).

Heat the oven to 400°F (200°C).

Dump the cooked spaghetti into 2 small ovenproof, individual-sized, serving dishes. Slice the cutlets into thin strips and heap on top of the spaghetti. Splash the sauce evenly over both dishes and sprinkle with Parmesan cheese. Bake in oven, uncovered, for 10 minutes.

Serves: 2

ZUCCHINI PARMESAN

1 tbsp.	butter	15 mL
1	medium zucchini, in ¼" (1.3 cm) slices	1
2 tbsp.	grated Parmesan cheese	30 mL
	salt and pepper, to taste	

Melt butter in frying pan, add zucchini and sauté over low heat until the zucchini is tender. Increase heat to high, sprinkle in the Parmesan cheese, salt and pepper and fry for 2 minutes. Serve.

Serves: 2

AU GRATIN POTATOES

3	potatoes, boiled until tender and diced	3
1 cup	cheese sauce, Cheez Whiz OR Cheddar cheese soup	250 mL
	salt and pepper, to taste	
2 tbsp.	bread crumbs	30 mL

Combine potatoes and cheese sauce in a pot and heat on medium until well-blended. Season with salt and pepper.

Scoop 2 portions into separate ovenproof dishes. Sprinkle bread crumbs on top and broil at 450°F (230°C) for 5 minutes until brown and bubbly.

Serves: 2

CHOCOLATE MOCHA DESSERT

1 cup	chocolate pudding	250 mL
1½ tsp.	instant coffee	7 mL
¼ cup	whipping cream, whipped OR topping	50 mL
2 tbsp.	chopped peanuts	30 mL
2	maraschino cherries	2

Blend chocolate pudding and coffee together. Dump even portions into 2 dessert dishes.

Garnish with whipped cream, peanuts and maraschino cherries.

Serves: 2

Hot Tomato Bouillon
Rock Cornish Game Hens
Wild Rice with Mushrooms
Asparagus Spears
Chocolate Custard Surprise

Wine — Sauvignon Blanc OR Beaujolais

EPT: 60 minutes

HOT TOMATO BOUILLON

¾ cup	V-8 juice	175 mL
¼ cup	water	50 mL
1	beef bouillon cube	1
1	celery stalk, finely diced	1

Throw everything together in a pot. Heat over medium-high heat until boiling, stirring occasionally.

Serves: 2

ROCK CORNISH GAME HENS
(with or without stuffing)

2	Rock Cornish game hens	2
dash	salt	dash
¼ cup	butter, melted	50 mL
¼ tsp.	Tabasco sauce	1 mL

Since you will probably be using frozen game hens, thaw them first. Heat oven to 350°F (180°C). Rinse out the inside of the hens with cold water, patting dry with a paper towel. Then rub the insides with salt.

Place the hens, breast side up, on a rack in a shallow roasting pan. Slosh the butter and Tabasco sauce together. Brush part of the butter concoction on the hens, then sprinkle the hens with salt. If using wild rice and mushroom mix as a stuffing (see following recipe now), stuff hens at this point.

Roast, uncovered, until tender (about 1 hour), brushing hens about 3-4 times with the butter concoction while roasting.

Serves: 2

110

WILD RICE WITH MUSHROOMS
(Stuffing or Side Dish)

1 cup	canned chicken broth OR use a bouillon cube	250 mL
⅓ cup	uncooked wild rice	75 mL
2 tbsp.	butter	30 mL
1 tbsp.	sliced almonds	15 mL
1 tbsp.	chopped onion	15 mL
handful	mushrooms, thinly sliced	handful

As stuffing: Take the chicken broth and wild rice and boil until the rice is tender, about 30 minutes. Drain liquid off, add the remaining ingredients and stuff into the hens.

As a side dish: Melt butter in a frying pan. Dump in rice, almonds and onions and cook until the almonds are golden brown, about 10 minutes. Then chuck in the mushrooms and chicken broth. Turn up heat until the concoction boils.

Throw the boiling rice mixture into an ungreased casserole dish. Cover and bake in an oven at 350°F (180°C) until all liquid is absorbed and rice is tender, about 1 hour.

Serves: 2

ASPARAGUS SPEARS

| 10 oz. | asparagus spears, fresh OR frozen | 284 g |
| ¼ cup | Italian dressing | 50 mL |

To cook fresh asparagus, put in boiling water, reduce heat and simmer for about 5 minutes. If frozen, cook according to package directions. While the asparagus cooks, heat up the Italian dressing in a small pot on medium heat.

Slosh the dressing over the asparagus just before serving.

Serves: 2

CHOCOLATE CUSTARD SURPRISE

4	squares sweet cooking chocolate, 1 oz. (30 g) each	4
1 tbsp.	sugar	15 mL
⅓ cup	whipping cream	75 mL
1	egg yolk*	1
¼ tsp.	vanilla	1 mL
¼ cup	whipping cream, whipped	50 mL

Cook chocolate, sugar and cream over medium heat, stirring constantly, until the chocolate has melted and the mixture is smooth.

Put the egg yolk in a bowl and beat gently. Take 1 tbsp. (15 mL) of the hot chocolate mixture and blend it with the egg yolk in the bowl. Stir it into the hot chocolate mixture.

Remove mixture from heat. Stir in the vanilla. Pour equal amounts into 2 small dessert dishes. Chill in refrigerator until cooled. Add whipped cream just before serving.

*See egg-separating instructions on page 80.

Serves: 2

111

Cabbage Vegetable Salad
Flambé Steak Diane
Potato Pancakes
Glazed Carrots
Cherries Jubilee

Wine — any red wine except Beaujolais

EPT: 60 minutes

CABBAGE VEGETABLE SALAD

¼	head cabbage, shredded	¼
2	carrots, shredded	2
1	beet, shredded	1
½	cucumber, seeded and sliced	½
2	radishes, sliced	2
1	tomato, sliced	1
¼ cup	French dressing	50 mL

Arrange vegetables in a deep salad bowl in circular heaps. Scatter sliced tomato over the entire combination. Just before serving, slop the French dressing over vegetables.

Serves: 2

FLAMBÉ STEAK DIANE

1½ tbsp.	vegetable oil (divided)	22 mL
2	green onions, chopped	2
1½ tbsp.	chopped parsley	22 mL
½ tsp.	Worcestershire sauce	2 mL
¼ tsp.	salt	1 mL
dash	pepper	dash
¼ cup	gravy (from package mix)	50 mL
4	beef tenderloin filets, 4 oz. (115 g) each	4
2 tbsp.	brandy	30 mL
2 tbsp.	red wine	30 mL

Heat ½ tbsp. (7 mL) of the vegetable oil over medium heat and sauté the onions for 1-2 minutes.

Add parsley, Worcestershire sauce, salt, pepper and gravy to this mixture. Stir well and then remove from heat.

In a second frying pan, sauté steaks over medium-high heat with remaining 1 tbsp. (15 mL) of vegetable oil, until done to your liking.

Slosh the brandy and red wine over the steaks. Touch the edge of the mixture in the pan with a lighted match. (Have fire extinguisher handy! No kidding!)

When the flames subside, spoon the onion sauce over the steaks, stir a bit, then serve . . . even if your date's name isn't Diane!

Serves: 2

POTATO PANCAKES

2 cups	water	500 mL
1 tsp.	lemon juice	5 mL
2	potatoes (1 raw grated, 1 boiled and mashed)	2
1	egg, beaten	1
2 tbsp.	milk	30 mL
½ tsp.	salt	2 mL
⅓ cup	vegetable oil	75 mL

Pour the water into a bowl and add the lemon juice. Slosh the grated potato, only, into the water, swirl it around, then drain off the water. Add the mashed potato, egg, milk and salt. Mix all these ingredients until smooth. Shape 2 patties from this mixture.

Heat the oil in a frying pan over medium heat. Drop the patties (pancakes) into the hot oil. When brown and firm on the bottom sides, flip them over. Brown the other side.

Remove, pat off excess grease with a paper towel. Keep heated in an oven at low heat, if necessary, or serve immediately.

Serves: 2

GLAZED CARROTS

2 cups	fresh or frozen carrots	500 mL
1 tbsp.	butter	15 mL
	salt and pepper, to taste	
1 tbsp.	honey	15 mL

Slice fresh carrots into a pot and just barely cover with water. Bring to a boil, reduce heat and simmer until they are tender (about 3-5 minutes). If carrots are frozen, cook according to the package directions.

When carrots are cooked, sauté them in a frying pan over medium heat with melted butter, salt, pepper and honey.

Serves: 2

CHERRIES JUBILEE

1 cup	red currant jelly	250 mL
2 tsp.	butter	10 mL
1 cup	canned Bing cherries, well-drained and pitted	250 mL
¼ cup	kirsch	50 mL
1 cup	vanilla ice cream (2 scoops)	250 mL

Melt jelly in frying pan. Add butter and stir until melted. Dump the cherries in and heat them thoroughly.

Slop kirsch over the cherries.

Keep that fire extinguisher handy!!

Ignite with a match and let it burn until flame dies. Stir several times.

Scoop even portions of ice cream (we know how sensitive some people are!) into 2 dessert bowls. Spoon sauce over each serving, don't even think about the calories, and serve.

Serves: 2

113

Broth with Beaten Egg
Beef 'n' Greens
Chicken Fried Rice
Fruit Cocktail Surprise

Wine — Cabernet Sauvignon OR Syrah

EPT: 60 minutes

BROTH WITH BEATEN EGG

2 cups	beef OR chicken broth (canned or from bouillon cubes)	500 mL
1	egg	1
1 tbsp.	grated Parmesan cheese	15 mL
2 tsp.	chopped parsley	10 mL

Bring broth to a boil in a medium-sized pot.

Beat egg, cheese and parsley together. Throw this mixture into the broth, stirring constantly with a fork.

Continue to stir and cook until egg has scrambled in the hot broth mixture. Pour into 2 soup bowls and serve immediately.

Serves: 2

BEEF 'N' GREENS

½ lb.	beef, thinly sliced (the more tender the better)	250 g
2	carrots, thinly sliced at an angle	2
1	garlic clove, peeled and crushed	1
2 tbsp.	soy sauce	30 mL
1½ tbsp.	sherry	22 mL
1 tbsp.	vegetable oil	15 mL
½	onion, diced	½
1	celery stalk, thinly sliced at an angle	1
½ lb.	broccoli florets	250 g

Marinate beef, carrots and garlic in a mixture of soy sauce and sherry for at least 6 hours before cooking. Stir several times during the marinating process to make sure all beef is saturated.

When ready to prepare the meal, heat the vegetable oil in a wok or frying pan at high heat. Strain the meat from the marinade and save the liquid. Dump the meat into the wok (or frying pan) and stir-fry for 1 minute.

Toss the remaining ingredients and the marinade (which we saved!) into the wok and continue to stir-fry until the vegetables are bright in color (approximately 3 minutes).

Serve immediately.

Serves: 2

CHICKEN FRIED RICE

2 tbsp.	vegetable oil	30 mL
¼	onion, finely diced	¼
¼	green pepper, finely diced	¼
1	egg	1
2 cups	cooked rice	500 mL
¼ cup	diced cooked chicken	50 mL
1 tbsp.	soy sauce	15 mL

Heat oil in a frying pan over medium-high heat. Heave onions and green pepper in and cook until brown. Toss the egg in and mix it around. Fling the remaining ingredients into the pan and continue cooking over medium heat, stirring frequently, for about 5 minutes.

Serves: 2

FRUIT COCKTAIL SURPRISE

1	egg, well beaten	1
1 cup	sugar	250 mL
1	orange, juice and grated rind of	1
1	lime, juice and grated rind of	1
1	lemon, juice and grated rind of	1
2 cups	diced fresh mixed fruit OR 14 oz. (398 mL) can fruit cocktail	500 mL

Dump egg, sugar, juices and all rind into a pot. If using fresh fruit, add ½ cup (125 mL) of any fruit juice to the egg mixture in the pot. If using canned fruit, drain the fruit and use that juice. Cook over medium heat, stirring constantly, until the concoction comes to a boil. Boil for 1 minute.

Remove from heat, cool for 10 minutes, and pour the contents into a covered jar. Store the jar of sauce in the refrigerator.

Just before serving, prepare equal portions of the fruit and drench with the sauce.

Serves: 2

Clarence Culpepper's Words of Wisdom: "If one of these intimate meals for two don't get her . . . she ain't worth gettin'!"

COOKING FOR SIX TO EIGHT

Who would have thought you'd ever have this many acquaintances ... let alone friends? Or that they'd all gather at your place and expect to be fed? On the same day at roughly the same time??

Never fear! The Bachelor's Guide is here.

Browse through the more than fifty nifty hints in the Appendix for some ideas on shopping, meal planning and preparation.

You'll find that cooking for more than two is like upping the ante in poker ... it shouldn't change how you play the game! But, if it does, avoid the stress by calling the caterer or changing your game ... or your address.

COOKING FOR SIX TO EIGHT

BAKED COD TAILS

1	large onion, sliced	1
2 handfuls	mushrooms, sliced	2 handfuls
2 tbsp.	butter	30 mL
12	cod tails*, 3-4 oz. (85-115 g) each	12
	salt and pepper, to taste	
½ cup	white wine	125 mL
2	tomatoes, sliced	2
1	lemon, sliced	1

Heat oven to 375°F (190°C).

Fry onions and mushrooms in butter over medium-high heat and set them aside.

Grease a baking sheet. Spread the cod tails evenly on baking sheet. Season them with salt and pepper. Throw the fried onions and mushrooms on top of each cod tail. Splash the wine over the fish. Bake for 20 minutes in your preheated oven.

Serve, garnished with sliced tomatoes and lemons, and a silly grin!

*Cod tails are the fleshy tail-end portion of a cod fillet. If unavailable, use cod fillets.

Serves: 6-8

EPT: 30 minutes

BEEF POT ROAST WITH VEGETABLES

¼ cup	butter	50 mL
3-4 lbs.	boneless roast	1.5-2 kg
	salt and pepper, to taste	
	garlic powder, to taste	
1	onion, diced	1
2	carrots, diced	2
4	celery stalks, diced	4
2 lbs.	potatoes, peeled and diced	1 kg
2 x 28 oz.	cans whole tomatoes	2 x 796 mL

Heat oven to 400°F (200°C).

Melt butter in a casserole dish that has a cover. Rub the roast with salt, pepper and garlic. Stick it in the casserole dish and pop it in the oven, uncovered. Turn the roast until all sides are browned, about 10 minutes per side.

Reduce the oven heat to 350°F (180°C) and cover the casserole dish. Cook for 1 hour, turning roast over after 30 minutes.

When the hour is up, throw in the vegetables and cook, covered, for 1½ hours.

To serve, slice beef and plop it on a warmed serving dish. Surround with the vegetables.

Serves: 6-8

EPT: 2½ hours

118

COQ AU VIN (CHICKEN IN WINE)

¼ cup	butter	50 mL
3 lbs.	chicken parts	1.5 kg
½ cup	flour	125 mL
4	bacon strips, diced	4
8	small white onions, diced	8
2 handfuls	mushrooms, quartered	2 handfuls
1	garlic clove, minced	1
¼ cup	brandy	50 mL
½ cup	red wine	125 mL
4 cups	gravy (from packaged mix)	1 L
1 tbsp.	chopped parsley	15 mL
1 tsp.	salt	5 mL
½ tsp.	pepper	2 mL

Place butter in a frying pan over medium heat. Dredge chicken parts in flour, brown lightly in the butter and then set aside. Throw the bacon, onions, mushrooms and garlic into the pan. Cook all these ingredients only until very lightly browned, then remove them with a slotted spoon and set them aside.

Chuck the brandy into the pan and set it on fire. When the flames die, dump in the wine, gravy, parsley, salt and pepper. Stir all these ingredients together, replace the chicken, cover and simmer for about 25 minutes, covered.

Now put all ingredients (chicken, veggie mix and wine sauce) into a large pot. Cover and cook over low heat for 30 minutes . . . or until chicken is fork tender * then serve.

* Fork tender means you can flake the chicken off the bone easily with a fork.

Serves: 6-8

EPT: 60 minutes

FETTUCCINE ALFREDO

6 portions	fettuccine, cooked	6 portions
2	egg yolks*	2
1½ cups	whipping cream	375 mL
½ lb.	butter	250 g
1 cup	Parmesan cheese	250 mL

Cook noodles according to instructions on package.

While noodles are cooking, beat egg yolks lightly with a whisk and add cream slowly.

Place the drained hot noodles in a large serving bowl. Add the egg and cream mixture, melted butter and the Parmesan cheese. Toss with a large fork and serve immediately.

*See page 80 for egg separation techniques.

Serves 6:

EPT: 30 minutes

119

LAMB CHOPS WITH ROSEMARY AND LEMON SAUCE

16	lamb rib chops, 3-4 oz. (85-115 g) each	16
4 tbsp.	vegetable oil	60 mL
1 cup	dry white wine	250 mL
2 tsp.	crushed rosemary	10 mL
¼ cup	lemon juice	50 mL
2 tsp.	Dijon mustard	10 mL
	salt, to taste	
1 tsp.	pepper	5 mL

Pat lamb chops dry with paper towels. Brush a large frying pan with the vegetable oil and heat on medium-high.

Add the lamb chops and fry for approximately 7 minutes on each side.

Remove chops and place on a serving platter. Keep 'em warm.

Pour the excess fat from the pan and put the pan back on the stove. Add the white wine and bring it to a boil, stirring up the brown bits from the bottom of the pan.

Add the rosemary, lemon juice and mustard. Reduce the liquid by evaporation (boil it down) . . . until it becomes syrupy.

Season the sauce with salt and pepper and serve over the chops.

Optional: This dish is excellent when accompanied by honey-glazed carrots and pan-fried baby potatoes.

Serves: 6-8

EPT: 45 minutes

WATCH OUT MY LI'L LAMBCHOPS — THAT'S THE INFAMOUS OL' ROSEMARY BO BEEP!

HAM IN RAISIN SAUCE

3 lbs.	boneless ham	1.5 kg
4 cups	apple juice	1 L
½ tsp.	cinnamon	2 mL
2 tbsp.	brown sugar	30 mL
1½ cups	raisins	375 mL
1 cup	cold water	250 mL
3 tbsp.	cornstarch	45 mL
1	orange, sliced	1

Heat oven to 375°F (190°C). Bake ham in a roasting pan for 45 minutes.

While the ham bakes, dump apple juice, cinnamon, brown sugar and raisins in a saucepan and simmer for 15 minutes. Meanwhile, mix cold water and cornstarch together until a smooth paste is formed.

Bring the raisin concoction to a boil and slowly add the cornstarch paste, stirring constantly until the mixture thickens. Simmer for another 10 minutes, stirring frequently. Keep on very low heat while ham is baking.

When ham is finished baking, remove from the oven, slice and throw onto a warm serving tray. Splash the raisin sauce over the top. Garnish with orange slices and serve.

Serves: 6-8

EPT: 90 minutes

PEROGIES AND SAUSAGES

24	perogies, fresh OR frozen	24
½ lb.	bacon, diced	250 g
1	onion, sliced	1
¼ cup	butter	50 mL
1 lb.	pork sausage links*	500 g
	salt and pepper, to taste	

Toss fresh perogies in a large pot of boiling water and cook until they float. Remove the perogies from the water after about 5 minutes. (If perogies are frozen, follow directions on the package.) Drain and then set them aside.

In a frying pan over medium heat, sauté bacon and onion in butter. Also, in yet another frying pan (we warned you about the single-ring hotplate!), fry the sausages.

Hurl the perogies in with the bacon and onion. Season to your own personal taste with salt and pepper. Shove these around for awhile.

Serve the perogies with the sausages and a tossed salad on the side.

*We've budgeted 2 sausages per person, but it really depends on the size of your friends and their appetites!

Serves: 6-8

EPT: 15 minutes

LASAGNE

13	lasagne noodles (approx. ¾ pkg.)	13
1 tbsp.	vegetable oil	15 mL
2	green peppers, diced	2
2	large onions, diced	2
2	celery stalks, diced	2
3	garlic cloves, minced	3
handful	mushrooms, sliced	handful
2 tbsp.	chopped parsley	30 mL
	salt and pepper, to taste	
½ lb.	ground beef	250 g
3 cups	tomato sauce	750 mL
½ cup	cottage cheese	125 mL
1	egg	1
½ lb.	mozzarella cheese, sliced	250 g

Cook lasagne noodles according to directions on the package.

Heat oven to 350°F (180°C). Heat vegetable oil in a frying pan over medium-high heat. Sauté peppers, onions, celery and garlic in the pan. Chuck in the mushrooms and parsley, then season with salt and pepper.

Heave in the ground beef and continue to sauté for 5 minutes. Finally, heap half the tomato sauce into the mess. Spread the other half over the bottom of an 8" x 12" (3 L) baking pan.

Arrange half of the cooked lasagne noodles on top of the sauce, covering the bottom of the pan. Spread half of the meat sauce over the noodles.

Mix cottage cheese and egg together and throw on top of the layer of meat sauce. Add half of the mozzarella cheese to the same layer.

Lay the remaining noodles lengthwise across the top.

Dump the remaining meat sauce and mozzarella cheese over the top. Bake for 35 minutes in your preheated oven.

Serve with candlelight and 2 Italian violinists for maximum effect!

Serves: 6-8

EPT: 60 minutes

PORK CHOPS AND MUSHROOMS

12	pork chops	12
½ cup	flour	125 mL
	salt and pepper, to taste	
2 tbsp.	vegetable oil	30 mL
2 tbsp.	butter	30 mL
2 handfuls	mushrooms, sliced	2 handfuls
2 x 10 oz.	mushroom soup (2 cans)	2 x 284 mL
1	soup can water OR milk	1

Heat oven to 375°F (190°C).

Flop chops in flour, season with salt and pepper, then fry in oil over medium-high heat until done, 4-6 minutes per side for ½" (1.5 cm) thick chops. Flip the cooked chops into a casserole dish.

Melt butter in a pot. Toss the mushrooms in and sauté until golden. Dump in the 2 cans of soup and the 1 can of liquid (water or milk). Bring to a boil and slosh over the top of the chops.

Bake in oven for 30 minutes.

Serve with mashed potatoes or rice.

Serves: 6-8

EPT: 45 minutes

TEMPTING DESSERTS

Warning! If you are counting calories, turn back now!!!

The following pages contain desserts to die for. Half the challenge is to create one without succumbing to the temptation to dive in prior to your guest's arrival.

It is definitely unfashionable to answer the door with impossible pie residue around one's professional puckers.

Those socially appropriate and responsible warnings out of the way . . . while you cannot have your cake and eat it, too . . . you can prepare a dangerous delight for your date at dessert and have a little cookie later with your special coffee!

HELLUVA WAY TO RUN A KITCHEN

TEMPTING DESSERTS

MOCHA PARFAITS

¼ cup	whipping cream, whipped	50 mL
2 tsp.	sugar	10 mL
½ tsp.	instant coffee	2 mL
½ cup	chocolate pudding	125 mL
1 tbsp.	chocolate chips	15 mL

In a chilled bowl (stick it in the freezer for 30 minutes), beat whipping cream, sugar and instant coffee until stiff enough that a fork stands up in it.

Alternate layers of pudding and the whipping cream concoction in parfait glasses or dessert dishes. Chill in refrigerator for 30 minutes.

Garnish with chocolate chips before serving.

Serves: 1-2

EPT: 45 minutes

CHOCOLATE MOUSSE

1 cup	chocolate pudding	250 mL
¼ cup	whipping cream	50 mL
¼ cup	whipping cream, whipped	50 mL
2	maraschino cherries	2

Take chocolate pudding and whipping cream and place in a mixing bowl and whip on high until well-blended and thick (about 4 minutes).

Put equal portions in dessert dishes or parfait glasses and top with whipped cream and maraschino cherries.

Optional: Chill in refrigerator for 30 minutes before serving.

Serves: 2

EPT: 15 minutes

126

CHOCOLATE PEARS

1	small can pear halves	1
1	small can chocolate pudding	1
2 tbsp.	peppermint schnapps liqueur	30 mL
½ cup	whipping cream, whipped	125 mL
2	maraschino cherries	2

Throw a couple of pear halves into each dessert dish. Plop the pudding into a bowl and stir the peppermint schnapps liqueur into the pudding.

Slosh the pudding over the pears. Garnish with whipped cream and a cherry.

Serves: 2

EPT: 10 minutes

RAINBOW PARFAITS

sherbets
ginger ale

Choose 2 or 3 flavors of sherbet, such as raspberry, pineapple, orange or lime (about 1 cup [250 mL] of each). Use a scoop to make small balls. Divide the scoops between 2 parfait glasses and throw them in the freezer.

At serving time, fill the parfait glasses with ginger ale.

Serves: 2

EPT: 5 minutes

PINEAPPLE SANDWICHES

1	small can pineapple rings, drained	1
2	scoops orange sherbet	2
2 tsp.	apricot jam	10 mL
2 tsp.	chopped walnuts	10 mL

Catapult a pineapple slice onto each dessert plate. Dump a scoop of sherbet on top.

Take another pineapple slice and crown the sherbet with it. Dribble the jam over each serving and sprinkle some walnuts on top.

Keep in the freezer until ready to serve.

Serves: 2

EPT: 5 minutes

VELVET CRUMB CAKE WITH PINEAPPLE SAUCE

⅓ cup	brown sugar	75 mL
2 tsp.	cornstarch	10 mL
¾ cup	crushed pineapple	175 mL
2	individual sponge cakes (available at the grocery store)	2
½ cup	whipping cream, whipped	125 mL
2	maraschino cherries, optional	2

Mix sugar and cornstarch in a small pot. Stir in the pineapple and the syrup from the can. Cook over medium heat, stirring constantly until the concoction thickens and boils. Let boil for 1 minute, stirring constantly.

Toss the sponge cakes onto dessert dishes and throw warm sauce over each. Top with whipped cream and, if you like, a maraschino cherry and serve.

Serves: 2

EPT: 15 minutes

IMPOSSIBLE PIE

5	eggs	5
½ cup	margarine	125 mL
1 cup	shredded coconut	250 mL
2 tsp.	vanilla	10 mL
½ cup	flour	125 mL
2 cups	milk	500 mL
1 cup	sugar	250 mL

Blend all ingredients in the blender.

Pour the entire concoction into a well-greased 10" (25 cm) glass pie plate.

Bake at 350°F (180°C) for approximately 1 hour.

Let pie stand on counter for approximately 1 hour. For best results, chill in refrigerator for an additional hour before serving.

Serves: 2

EPT: 2 hours

CHERRY BOSTON CREAM PIE

½ cup	graham cracker crumbs	125 mL
½ cup	cherry pie filling	125 mL
¼ cup	whipping cream, whipped	50 mL
½ cup	drained crushed pineapple	125 mL
½ cup	miniature marshmallows	125 mL

Take 2 dessert dishes and place graham cracker crumbs in the bottom of each. (Reserve about 2 tsp. (10 mL) of crumbs to garnish the top of each dessert.) Then top each layer of crumbs with ¼ cup (50 mL) of cherry pie filling.

In a separate bowl, combine the whipped cream, pineapple and marshmallows. Divide this confection between each dessert dish, sprinkle the top with additional graham cracker crumbs and serve.

Optional: Chill for 30 minutes before serving.

Serves: 2

EPT: 15 minutes

FLAMBÉ CRÊPES SUZETTE

Crêpe Mix:

½ cup	all-purpose flour	125 mL
1 tsp.	sugar	5 mL
¼ tsp.	baking powder	1 mL
¼ tsp.	salt	1 mL
⅔ cup	milk	150 mL
1	egg	1
¼ tsp.	vanilla	1 mL
2 tsp.	butter, melted	10 mL

To make the crêpes:

Using an egg beater, whip all ingredients together until smooth. For each crêpe . . . lightly butter an 8" (20 cm) skillet then heat over medium heat until butter is bubbly.

Pour ¼ cup (50 mL) of the batter into skillet. Immediately rotate pan until batter covers the bottom. Cook until light brown. Flip the crêpe over and brown other side. Stack crêpes so "first-baked" side is down and slip wax paper between each crêpe to prevent them from sticking together. Cover stack of crêpes with wax paper to prevent them from drying out.

Sauce Mix:

¼ cup	butter	50 mL
¼ tsp.	grated orange peel	1 mL
¼ cup	orange juice	50 mL
1 tbsp.	sugar	15 mL
2 tbsp.	orange-flavored liqueur OR brandy	30 mL
1	fire extinguisher (keep it handy!!)	1

To make the sauce:

Heat on high, butter, orange peel, orange juice and sugar to boiling, stirring occasionally. Let it boil for 1 minute stirring constantly . . . then reduce heat to medium.

Fold crêpes in half and in half again (for a pie wedge shape) and then place them in the hot orange sauce. Turn crêpes once. Pour in the orange liqueur and ignite with a match. When flames subside, place 2 crêpes on each dessert plate and spoon the sauce over them.

Serves: 2

EPT: 20 minutes

If this doesn't impress your dinner companion, tell her your French maid, Suzette, loved them!

BAKED APPLES

2	apples	2
2-3 tbsp.	brown sugar	30-45 mL
2 tsp.	margarine	10 mL
dash	cinnamon	dash
2 tsp.	syrup (maple, corn, etc.)	10 mL

Heat oven to 350°F (180°C).

Core the apples and peel off 1" (2.5 cm) of skin around the middle of each apple, or peel the upper half of each apple, to prevent them from splitting during baking.

Place each apple upright in a small baking dish. Fill center of each apple with 1-2 tbsp. (15-30 mL) brown sugar, 1 tsp. (5 mL) margarine, a dash of cinnamon and 1 tsp. (5 mL) syrup.

Dump about ¼" (0.5 cm) of water into each baking dish. Bake in the oven until the apples are tender when pierced with a fork, about 30-40 minutes.

For extra flavor, spoon the pan syrup over the apples several times while baking.

Serves: 2

EPT: 45 minutes

ROSY CINNAMON APPLES

2	apples	2
2 tbsp.	brown sugar	30 mL
1 tbsp.	red cinnamon candies	15 mL

Heat oven to 350°F (180°C).

Remove the cores from the apples. Peel the upper half of each apple to prevent splitting.

Place apples upright in a small baking dish. Fill center of each with 1 tbsp. (15 mL) brown sugar and 1½ tsp. (7 mL) of red cinnamon candies.

Throw about ¼" (0.5 cm) water into the baking dish. Bake until apples are tender when pierced with a fork, about 30-40 minutes. Serve warm.

Serves: 2

EPT: 50 minutes

Frau "Ingie" Culpepper's advice to bachelors: He who marries for money earns every penny!

131

APPLE CRISP

19 oz.	can apple pie filling	540 mL
1 tbsp.	water	15 mL
½ tsp.	lemon juice	2 mL
½ tsp.	cinnamon	2 mL
¼ cup	brown sugar	50 mL
3 tbsp.	flour	45 mL
2 tbsp.	butter	30 mL

Heat oven to 350°F (180°C).

Heave apple pie filling into an ungreased casserole dish. Throw the water, lemon juice and cinnamon over the apples.

Mix brown sugar, flour and butter until crumbly and then dump this sweet treat on top of the apples.

Bake, uncovered, until apples are tender and topping is golden brown, about 30 minutes. Top with ice cream and serve.

Serves: 2

EPT: 40 minutes

PEACH CRISPS

4	canned peach halves	4
2 tbsp.	chopped walnuts	30 mL
2 tbsp.	brown sugar	30 mL
1½ tsp.	finely grated orange peel	7 mL
dash	allspice	dash
1 tbsp.	graham cracker crumbs	15 mL
4	walnut halves	4
	vanilla ice cream, optional	

Heat oven to 350°F (180°C). Place peach halves, cut sides up, in greased baking dish.

In another bowl, mix walnuts, sugar, orange peel, allspice and graham cracker crumbs together. Sprinkle this confection on the peaches.

Bake until heated through, about 20 minutes. Serve warm. Top each piece with a walnut half and, if you like, a scoop of vanilla ice cream.

Serves: 2

EPT: 30 minutes

WARM PEACH CRUNCH SUNDAES

14 oz.	can peach halves, drained	398 mL
2 tbsp.	brown sugar	30 mL
¼ cup	crushed cashews	50 mL
1 tbsp.	butter OR margarine	15 mL
2	scoops vanilla ice cream	2

Set oven temperature control at broil . . . or 550°F (290°C). Plunk peaches into an 8" (20 cm) ovenproof skillet or shallow baking dish.

Pitch the sugar and cashews over the peaches, then dot with butter.

Broil about 6" (15 cm) from the heat for about 2 minutes — until sugar and butter are melted and the sauce is bubbly. Serve immediately over ice cream.

Serves: 2

EPT: 15 minutes

SPICED FRUIT

| 14 oz. | can fruit cocktail | 398 mL |
| dash | allspice | dash |

Heat fruit cocktail in its juice over medium-high heat. Sprinkle in the allspice and continue to cook until it boils. Then serve.

Serves: 2

EPT: 2 minutes

RAISIN BREAD PUDDING

2	bread slices, cut in 1" (2.5 cm) cubes	2
1 tbsp.	butter OR margarine	15 mL
1	egg	1
⅔ cup	milk	150 mL
3 tbsp.	brown sugar	45 mL
⅓ cup	raisins	75 mL
½ tsp.	cinnamon	2 mL
¼ tsp.	nutmeg	1 mL
dash	salt	dash

Heat oven to 350°F (180°C). Throw bread cubes into a casserole dish coated with the butter.

In another bowl, beat the egg slightly, then stir in the milk, brown sugar, raisins and seasonings. Slosh the egg mixture over the bread cubes.

Set the entire dish inside a baking pan, filled halfway with water. Bake for about 40 minutes or until a knife inserted in the center comes out clean. Serve warm.

Serves: 2

EPT: 50 minutes

INEXPENSIVE PARTY TREATS

INEXPENSIVE
PARTY TREATS

DILL PICKLE DIP

2 cups	sour cream	500 mL
2 tbsp.	chopped dill pickle	30 mL
1 tbsp.	pickle juice	15 mL
	lemon juice, to taste	

Toss all ingredients into a bowl. Slosh together and let stand for 2 hours, refrigerated, to blend flavors.

Yield: approximately 2 cups (500 mL).

GARLIC CHEESE DIP

2 cups	sour cream	500 mL
1	pkg. garlic cheese salad dressing mix	1

Dump both ingredients into a bowl. Pound them together and let the compound stand for 2 hours, refrigerated, to blend flavors.

Yield: approximately 2 cups (500 mL).

ONION DIP

2 cups	sour cream	500 mL
1	pkg. instant onion soup mix	1

Throw ingredients into a bowl. Mix them up well and let the mixture stand for 2 hours, refrigerated, to blend flavors.

Yield: approximately 2 cups (500 mL).

BBQ BUTTER

Stir 1 tsp. (5 mL) BBQ sauce into ¼ cup (50 mL) melted butter. Then pour over popcorn, toss around and serve.

DILL BUTTER

Dribble ¼ cup (50 mL) melted butter over the popcorn, sprinkle with 2 tsp (10 mL) of finely chopped dill weed. Toss popcorn before serving.

PARMESAN BUTTER

Stir 1 tbsp. (15 mL) grated Parmesan cheese into ¼ cup (50 mL) melted butter. Slosh over popcorn, toss and serve.

137

CHEESE TRAY

Choose different kinds of cheese . . . Camembert, Brie, Swiss, medium Cheddar, Gouda, or whatever you like.

Slice the cheese into different shapes (cubes, squares, triangles) and place on a tray, together with different kinds and shapes of crackers.

For variety's sake, get some frilled toothpicks, green pitted olives, cherry tomatoes, black olives and pickles. Jam a toothpick through 1 of these little vegi-doodles and stick it into a cube of cheese. Mini-kabobs!

FRUIT TRAY

	lettuce leaves	
½ lb.	grapes (2 varieties)	250 g
2-4	oranges	2-4
½	cantaloupe	½
½	honeydew	½
2 cups	watermelon chunks	500 mL
14 oz.	can sliced pineapple, drained	398 mL
	bananas, peaches, or whatever is in season	

Cover the bottom of the tray with lettuce leaves. Cut fruit into small pieces.

Fruits such as bananas, pears, peaches and apples will darken unless you soak the pieces for several minutes in a mixture of 1 cup (250 mL) water and 2 tbsp. (30 mL) lemon juice. Drain well.

Arrange the fruit on the tray so that no 2 pieces of the same fruit are side by side. Put a container of toothpicks at the side of the tray.

Serves: 4-6

MEAT TRAY

Select a variety of sliced meats . . . salami, ham, roast beef, turkey roll, corned beef, etc.

Cover the bottom of the tray with lettuce. Place the meat on the tray, either in rows or in circles.

Garnish the meat tray with tomato wedges and parsley sprigs between the rows of meat.

Uncle Yardley Culpepper's Hint to Would-Be Homebodies: Nothing pleases a man more than being mistaken for a football player.

VEGETABLE TRAY

Choose a selection of raw vegetables, such as broccoli, cauliflower, carrots, celery, radishes, cucumbers, cherry tomatoes and mushrooms. Break or cut vegetables into bite-size chunks.

Place a bowl of dip in the middle of the tray and arrange the vegetables around it.

Use one of the following dips. . .

CHEATER'S DIP

Thousand Island Salad Dressing OR
French Salad Dressing OR
Blue Cheese Salad Dressing OR
Italian Salad Dressing

Just pour a little in a nice bowl and serve, you cheapskate!

CREAMY ITALIAN DIP

| 1 cup | sour cream | 250 mL |
| ½ cup | Italian Dressing | 125 mL |

Chuck the sour cream and Italian Dressing into a bowl. Mash these 2 ingredients together and let the compound stand, refrigerated, for 30 minutes to blend flavors.

Yield: approximately 1½ cups (375 mL).

HORSERADISH SOUR CREAM DIP

1 cup	sour cream	250 mL
1 tsp.	prepared horseradish	5 mL
¼ tsp.	celery seed	1 mL

Slop ingredients together in a bowl. Let stand, refrigerated, for 2 hours to blend flavors.

Yield: approximately 1 cup (250 mL).

SPICY DIP

14 oz.	canned tomatoes, drained and chopped	398 mL
1 cup	chopped green onions	250 mL
1 tsp.	salt	5 mL
½ cup	green chili sauce	125 mL

Dump tomatoes, green onions and salt together. Throw some green chili sauce into the mess. Let this steamy concoction stand in refrigerator for 2 hours before using.

Yield: 1 cup (250 mL)

139

BIG DIPPERS

Any of the following work well as dippers. . .

> **French bread cubes**
> **cubed cooked ham**
> **peeled cooked shrimp**
> **cherry tomatoes**
> **green pepper strips**
> **cauliflower florets**
> **broccoli florets**
> **avocado slices**

Spread dippers attractively on several serving platters.

CHEESE AND BEER FONDUE

1 lb.	Cheddar cheese, grated	500 g
1 lb.	Monterey Jack cheese, grated	500 g
¼ cup	all-purpose flour	50 mL
2 tsp.	chili powder	10 mL
1	garlic clove, halved	1
12 oz.	bottle beer	341 mL
4 oz.	can hot green chili peppers, seeded and chopped	115 mL

Throw cheese together with flour and chili powder into a big bowl and blend well.

Rub the garlic half along the inside of the fondue pot. Dump beer into pot and heat slowly, until beer begins to bubble. Gradually add the cheese concoction, a handful at a time, stirring constantly, until cheese has melted and is smooth. Toss in the hot peppers. Serve fondue warm, together with your choice of "dippers".

CHINESE FONDUE

6 cups	chicken stock (canned broth)	1.5 L
2	medium carrots, thinly sliced	2
1	leek, finely sliced	1
1	celery stalk, thinly sliced	1
2 tbsp.	chopped parsley	30 mL

Dump chicken stock into fondue pot and throw pot onto stove. Toss in the carrots, leek, celery and parsley and bring to a boil, then reduce to low heat and simmer for 20 minutes.

While it cooks, you have time to prepare the sauces. . .

KETCHUP SAUCE

5 tbsp.	mayonnaise	75 mL
2 tbsp.	ketchup	30 mL
1 tsp.	Worcestershire sauce	5 mL
1 tsp.	curry powder	5 mL
dash each	sugar and salt	dash

Mash first 4 ingredients together. Season to taste with sugar and salt.

TARTAR SAUCE

5 tbsp.	mayonnaise	75 mL
2 tbsp.	capers, drained*	30 mL
2 tbsp.	chopped chives OR green onion	30 mL
2	dill pickles, finely chopped	2
2 tsp.	lemon juice	10 mL
2 tsp.	milk	10 mL
¼ tsp.	salt	1 mL
dash each	pepper, sugar	dash

Slosh first 6 ingredients together. Season to taste with salt and pepper.

* Check the pickle section at the grocery store to find capers.

To be dipped. . .

2 lbs.	lean beef, cut into paper-thin slices	1 kg

Pat meat dry with paper towel before putting on serving tray.

Place fondue pot with chicken broth on burner in middle of table. Make sure that broth continues to simmer. If broth evaporates too much, replenish with boiling water.

Roll up a slice of beef, place on your fondue fork and dump into chicken broth. Cook meat to your liking, then dunk into your favorite sauce . . . and enjoy.

For an added touch, when all beef has been eaten, ladle broth into bowls and serve.

141

JAPANESE FONDUE

6-8	wieners (hot dogs)	6-8
4	pimientos	4
4	small onions	4
1 lb.	beef, cubed	500 g
handful	mushrooms	handful
	vegetable oil (enough for deep frying)	

Chop hot dogs into 1" (2.5 cm) pieces. Cut pimientos into 2-3 small pieces each. Slice onion into wide rings. Arrange beef cubes, sliced hot dogs, pimientos, onions and whole mushrooms on a serving platter.

Pour vegetable oil into the fondue pot and heat over medium heat. When heated (check this by dropping a piece of food in the oil . . . if it bubbles, it's ready), set fondue pot on table, together with serving platter and sauces . . . Worcestershire sauce, lemon juice, mayonnaise and ketchup sauce.

Using fondue fork, pick up one ingredient at a time, dunk it in, and deep fry until done. Then dip it in any of the sauces and enjoy each and every morsel.

CHOCOLATE FONDUE DIP

(Try this one for dessert after one of the other fondues!)

	assorted fresh fruit pieces	
5	regular-size milk chocolate bars	5
1 cup	whipping cream	250 mL
¼ cup	brandy	50 mL

Peel and dice fruit. Fruit such as apples should be soaked in lemon/water, see Fruit Tray on page 138. Arrange the fruit on a tray and chill in the refrigerator until ready to serve.

Break the chocolate into small pieces and dump the pieces into a small saucepan. Throw in the cream and cook over low heat, stirring constantly, until the confection has melted and is smooth.

Then add the brandy and mix thoroughly.

Transfer mixture to fondue pot and keep it over low heat so the dip does not boil.

142

Usually a few munchies will do when the guys come over to watch TV sports and tell a few lies to each other.

Since you never know when an impromptu party may start, it pays to have an emergency cupboard full of chips, pretzels, popcorn, tacos, etc. . . .

This avoids last minute runs to expensive "convenience" stores which cause you to miss the first few minutes of the game. All your buddies have to bring are themselves and the beer.

Speaking of beer, it helps to have a few cold ones on hand. Whether you are "Mr. Maltster" and brew your own . . . (it can be done quite inexpensively . . . check the kits!) or expect your pals to sling their own suds over . . . variety is the spice of life in the hops department, too.

Have each guest bring a six-pack from a different brewery or country. You'll be pleasantly surprised at the unusual flavors. Beer at the BBQ, seafood surprise, with a pizza, or a few peanuts . . .   Expand your hops horizons. You'll be glad you did and acquire quite a cosmopolitan reputation to boot!

FORMAL PARTY TREATS
(when you have time to prepare)

ANGELS ON HORSEBACK

10	**bacon slices**	**10**
20	**smoked oysters**	**20**
20	**wooden toothpicks**	**20**

Cut the bacon slices in half. Roll each oyster in a half slice of bacon, and secure with a toothpick. Broil under medium heat until golden brown and serve with cocktail sauce.

Yield: 20 appetizers

EPT: 20 minutes

DEVILS ON HORSEBACK

10	**bacon slices**	**10**
20	**chicken livers**	**20**
20	**wooden toothpicks**	**20**

Cut the bacon slices in half. Roll each chicken liver in a half slice of bacon and secure with a toothpick. Broil under medium heat until golden brown and serve with cocktail sauce.

Yield: 20 appetizers

EPT: 20 minutes

143

PIGGIES IN A BLANKET

10	sausage links, cooked	10
10	bacon slices	10
20	wooden toothpicks	20

Cut the sausages and bacon in half. Roll each sausage in a half slice of bacon and secure with a toothpick.

Broil at medium heat until golden brown and serve with cocktail sauce.

Yield: 20 appetizers

EPT: 20 minutes

PINEAPPLE BACONS

10	bacon slices	10
20	fresh or canned pineapple chunks, cut in ½" (1.25 cm) cubes	20
20	wooden toothpicks	20

Cut each bacon slice in half and wrap around each pineapple cube.

Secure each with a toothpick and broil at medium until golden brown.

Serve with cocktail sauce.

Yield: 20 appetizers

EPT: 20 minutes

LEMON SOY CHICKEN WINGS

2 lbs.	chicken wings	1 kg
⅓ cup	soy sauce	75 mL
¼ cup	vegetable oil	50 mL
	juice from half a lemon	

Cut off the tips of the wings and discard. Cut the remaining chicken at the joint into 2 parts. Place these in a bowl.

Combine the remaining ingredients. Pour this mixture over the wings.

Let the wings marinate for at least 2 hours at room temperature . . . mixing twice during that time.

Place the wings on a baking sheet and bake in oven at 350°F (180°C) for 30 minutes, turning over once after 15 minutes and basting several times during cooking.

Serves: 4-6

EPT: 45 minutes

DILLY CHERRY TOMATOES

4 cups	cherry tomatoes	1 L
8 oz.	cream cheese	225 g
2 tbsp.	sour cream	30 g
2 tbsp.	lemon juice	30 g
¼ cup	fresh dill, chopped or 1-2 tbsp. (15-30 mL) of dillweed	50 mL

Cut a thin slice from the top of each tomato, scoop out the pulp, and sprinkle salt on the inside.

In a small bowl, mix the cream cheese, sour cream, lemon juice and dill until smooth. Spoon (or pipe with a pastry bag) this mixture into each prepared tomato and serve.

This treat may be prepared 6-8 hours in advance.

Serves: 8-10

EPT: 30 minutes

SCREWS AND NAILS

2 cups	Corn Chex	500 mL
2 cups	Rice Chex	500 mL
2 cups	Wheat Chex	500 mL
¾ cup	salted mixed nuts	175 mL
¾ cup	pretzel sticks	175 mL
6 tbsp.	margarine	90 mL
1 tsp.	seasoning salt	5 mL
4 tsp.	Worcestershire sauce	20 mL

Heat the oven to 250°F (120°C). Heat the margarine in a large, shallow baking pan until melted. Remove the pan from the heat. Stir in seasoning salt and Worcestershire sauce. Add Chex, nuts, and pretzel sticks.

Mix until all pieces are coated. Heat in the oven for 45 minutes. Stir every 15 minutes.

Spread on paper towels to absorb excess grease and to cool the mixture.

Yield: 7 cups (1.5 L)

EPT: 1 hour

146

FIVE-MINUTE FUDGE

⅔ cup	evaporated milk	150 mL
1⅔ cups	sugar	400 mL
½ tsp.	salt	2 mL
1½ cups	miniature marshmallows	375 mL
1½ cups	chocolate chips	375 mL
1 tsp.	vanilla	5 mL
½ cup	chopped walnuts	125 mL

Grease a 9" x 9" (23 x 23 cm) pan.

Mix milk, sugar and salt in a saucepan. Heat to a rolling boil and cook at this level for 5 minutes.

Remove from heat. Add the marshmallows, chocolate chips, vanilla and walnuts. Stir 1-2 minutes. Pour this entire mixture into the baking pan.

Let the mixture cool on the counter for at least 1 hour. Then refrigerate for an additional hour.

Serves: 10-12 or 2 sweet teeth

EPT: 5 minutes

SKILLET PEANUT BUTTER FUDGE

2 cups	sugar	500 mL
3 tbsp.	margarine	45 mL
1 cup	evaporated milk	250 mL
1 cup	miniature marshmallows	250 mL
1½ cups	peanut butter	375 mL
1 tsp.	vanilla	5 mL

In a frying pan, over medium-high heat, combine the sugar, margarine and milk. Bring this mixture to a boil and let it boil for 5 minutes. Stir constantly.

Turn off heat. Add the rest of the ingredients. Stir well.

Pour this confection into an 8" x 8" (20 x 20 cm) pan. Let it stand on the counter for 1 hour. Then place in the refrigerator to chill for another hour before serving.

Serves: 10-12

EPT: 10 minutes

POPCORN BALLS

3½ cups	popped popcorn	875 mL
1 cup	corn syrup	250 mL
½ cup	brown sugar	125 mL
2 tbsp.	margarine	30 mL

Pop the popcorn and place it in a large mixing bowl.

Mix the syrup, brown sugar and margarine in a pan and bring this mixture to a boil. When ready* pour the syrup slowly over the popcorn. Stir it all together. Dip your hands in cold water and then shape the popcorn into balls. Let the popcorn balls cool off. Serve when they harden.

*THE READY TEST is to take a drop of syrup and place it in cold water. If the drop hardens, the syrup is "ready"

Serves: 2-4

EPT: 10 minutes

WHIPPED SHORTBREAD

1 cup	margarine	250 mL
¼ cup	cornstarch	50 mL
½ cup	icing sugar	125 mL
1½ cups	flour	375 mL
	green and red glazed cherries, to personal taste	

Heat oven to 325°F (160°C).

Cream the margarine at low speed in the blender. **Gradually** beat in the cornstarch and then **gradually** beat in the other ingredients. Then turn the blender on high until the mixture is like whipping cream.

Test-bake 1 cookie for 15 - 20 minutes. If it is too "gooey", your mixture needs a bit more flour.

Drop globs of mixture on a cookie sheet or use a cookie cutter for fancy shapes. Pieces of cut cherries can be put on each cookie.

Bake for 15 - 20 minutes.

Yield: approximately 24 cookies

EPT: 1 hour

GINGERY TEA

6 cups	unsweetened pineapple juice	1.5 L
½ cup	brown sugar	125 mL
	cinnamon sticks	
1	fresh ginger root, 4" (10 cm), peeled and sliced	1
3 cups	hot tea (strong)	750 mL
	lemon slices, to taste	

In a saucepan combine pineapple juice, brown sugar, cinnamon sticks and ginger.

Simmer for 5 minutes to blend flavors. Add tea and heat to a boil.

Remove cinnamon and ginger. Serve in warm mugs garnished with lemon slices.

Yield: 11 cups (2.5 L)

EPT: 7 minutes

PARTY-PLEASER PUNCH

4 cups	hot tea	1 L
½ cup	sugar	125 mL
1½ cups	unsweetened white grape juice	375 mL
1 cup	orange juice	250 mL
½ cup	lemon juice	125 mL
2 x 10 oz.	cans of ginger ale, chilled	2 x 284 mL
	orange and lemon slices, to taste	

In a medium bowl, combine hot tea and sugar and mix until the sugar is dissolved.

In a punch bowl combine the tea and grape, orange, and lemon juices. Chill until serving.

Just before serving add ginger ale. Pour over ice in tall glasses. Garnish each glass with lemon and orange slices and let several slices float in the bowl as well.

Yield: 11 cups (2.5 L)

EPT: 5 minutes

Prison Chaplain Charles "The Charmer" Culpepper's Homily on Sensible and Sensitive Hospitality: Since not all of your friends will be outrageously addicted to alcohol and inarticulation, the perfect host keeps a collection of soft drinks, juices, and mineral water on hand for those with tastes that run counter to the popcorn and twist-top crowd.

FRUIT OF THE VINE ... WINES

APPENDIX A: FRUIT OF THE VINE — WINES

WHAT GOES WITH WHAT?

North Americans talk dry wine and drink sweet wine. The most popular wine today is a "German-style" white with a sweetness factor of two or three. However, the wine enthusiast almost always acquires a taste for both the drier reds and a wider range of whites.

People always want to know "which wine fits this meal?". There are no rules, guys, only guidelines. Robust wines, for example, might be a little overpowering for an aperitif (drink before dinner), but rise to the occasion if accompanied with food, especially cheeses.

Should you splurge on a very expensive wine we would recommend only an intimate friend, a little cheese, and a long, crusty French loaf.

Cooling a white wine enhances its crisp clean flavor.

Red wines, however, are more agreeable at or just below room temperature. Beaujolais, a red wine, may be enjoyed either way.

TASTING

Just before your next sip of wine, take time to. . .

SEE Look closely at the wine. Depth of color often indicates the wine's "body" or robustness. Grasping the wine glass by the stem, hold it up to the light and study the wine. How would you describe its color? If a white wine, is it a deep gold or light straw color? If red, is it soft "strawberry" or ruby red? Check for clarity. Muddy or dull-looking wines often taste that way. Clarity is a sign of wine in good condition.

SWIRL Swirl the wine gently around the glass. This action releases the aroma by bringing oxygen in contact with the wine.

SMELL Put your nose right up to the edge of the glass and inhale deeply. Concentrate on what you smell. Which aromas do you recognize? Fruit? Spices? Flowers, earth or herbs? Try to be scientific and identify which aromas you may recognize. If the wine smells dirty or "vinegary", or "chemical", something may have gone wrong during the wine-making or while the wine was in storage.

SIP Take a sip of wine, together with as much air as you can (the air you take enhances the flavor of the wine). Don't swallow. Instead. . .

SAVOR Let the wine roll over your tongue from one side of your mouth to the other. What does it feel like on your tongue? Smooth? Light? Heavy? Does it have one dominant flavor — or many? Are the flavors similar to, or different from, the wine's aroma? If it tastes, flat, stale, dirty, or has a chemical smell — don't drink it. You probably have a bad bottle.

SWALLOW Swallow the wine. Does the flavor linger, change or disappear? The better the wine, the longer and more intense the flavor.

152

BUYING

Check your favorite wine store for new and different wines. Bargain bins are a great source of new grape experiences. You find good wines in strange bottles with wild names and reasonable prices. As soon as a wine is recognized and appreciated — the price rises. So check the bargain bins!

Store wine on its side. This keeps the cork moist and seals the wine against air which, over time, could affect the flavor.

WHITES

SPARKLING (CHAMPAGNE METHOD)

These sparkling ("bubbly") wines are dry (brut) alternatives to their expensive cousins from Champagne, a grape-producing area of France.

Sparkling wines are perfect for before dinner or special occasions, with les hors d'oeuvres, or with any dessert. For a touch of class, keep the bottle in a bucket of ice between refills. Check Australia's new sparkling wines. They are little known and competitively priced — for a while.

RIESLING (pronounced "Reesling")

The Riesling wines (named after an area in Germany) have a unique sugar/acid balance. Riesling wines often have a honeyed/flowery flavor with a hint of herbaceous mint.

Rieslings are soft, fresh white wines that are delicious at lunchtime. This wine goes well with seafoods such as shrimp (or prawns), crab, or fish. Again, check the bargain bin for Australian and Canadian labels and get good taste at a great price.

ITALIAN WINES

Bolla Soave or Orvieto Classico from Ruffino are a blend of several grapes. These wines are fruity and can be either soft or dry. They go well with lighter pasta dishes and seafoods.

SAUVIGNON BLANC (pronounced "Soveeneo Blonk")

The sauvignon grape is often blended to produce wines of good value. The wine's abundant acid tends to give it a tart finish. It has a fruity, spicy taste. Richer sauvignon is aged in a slightly toasted barrel and produces the fume or "smoked" style.

These wines best accompany cold plates, seafood bisques and quiches.

CHARDONNAY

Perhaps the world's most sophisticated dry white wine, chardonnay is very difficult to find at reasonable prices. When chardonnay is aged in oak, the wine is in the "chablis-style". The name "chablis" has been wrongly used outside of France and often such mislabelled wines bear no resemblance to the character of a true chablis. Chablis has a steely, flinty mineral flavor. If aged in oak, the wood changes the aroma and taste of the chardonnay making it rich, woody, or slightly smoky. Chablis is great with shellfish. The heavier style of chardonnay works well with escargot, salmon and lobster dishes.

153

REDS

BEAUJOLAIS (pronounced Bow-shell-eh)

This wine has the aroma of strawberry jam. The flavor of a fresh beaujolais bursts forth. This red wine has virtually no tannins and loses its fresh charm as it ages. Beaujolais has much in common with white wine and is a pleasant addition to chicken, hamburger, cheese, or just about any food.

Every November try:
> **Beaujolais Nouveau** (France)
> **Beaujolais Villages** (France)

PINOT NOIR (pronounced Pee-no No-are)

Wines from Bordeaux (see below) are deep red. The Burgundies are more brillant, but age more quickly. The tannins in Pinot Noir are usually fairly light. Pinot noirs are difficult to describe. They have a sweet bouquet and a cedar wood, prune-like fruity taste. Pinots are just fine by themselves and go well with game birds.

CABERNET SAUVIGNON (pronounced Cab-er-nay-Sow-vin-knee-on)

The great French Bordeauxs are made predominantly from the Cabernet grape. Cabernets are deep ruby. Usually the bouquet can be either "oaky" or "cedary". The better cabernets are very intense. It helps to let them age for a while.

RIOJA (pronounced Rio-ha)

Spanish Rioja is perhaps the best value in red wine today. Reserves are partially aged and have a soft, vanilla, oaky, fruit flavor. Rioja is perfect for lamb, beef, pork, game meats, stews and casseroles. If you have spent your budget on food, whatever is left should be spent on Rioja. Look for the square Rioja stamp on the label.

CHIANTI/RUBESCO/BAROLO (Not to be confused with the Italian law firm of the same name!)

Chianti was one of the world's first dry red wines. In its youth it kisses, bites, thrusts and stings the palate . . . like you and your first real girlfriend! The reserves, however, can be velvety smooth. Try Frescobaldi's Chianti Rufina Remole with spicy dishes.

A **Rubusco** from Lungarotti has a more balanced body than Chianti.

Pio Cesare's Barolos are full-bodied Italian wines . . . similar to Italian women! As you may have guessed, Italian wines go well with Italian-style foods.

SYRAH (pronounced Se-rah)

These are full-bodied wines. Their slightly higher alcohol content make them warm, full wines with stews and casseroles. Most Côtes du Rhône Villages (France) are good choices.

154

YOUR OWN PRIVATE WINE CELLAR

Take the guesswork and last minute anxiety out of your wine shopping. When you find a wine that works well for you . . . make a note of it. Jot down the name, country, price and whatever comments will remind you of where and why that wine works well. Putting your feelings about the wine into words increases your vocabulary and familiarity with the flavor. Test each new wine as described earlier in the chapter . . . See, Swirl, Smell, Sip, Savor, Swallow . . . and get to know your local wine merchant. He or she will keep an eye out for new and interesting wines for you to try.

Wine	Country	Price	Flavor	Comments

Wine —

Wine —

Wine —

Wine —

Wine —

Wine —

Wine —

Wine —

Wine —

Wine —

155

APPENDIX B: GETTING STARTED

COOKING TOOLS AND TERMS

In any work or recreational activity, there are certain tools and terms to learn to make it as enjoyable as it can be for you and others. I've listed the cooking terms for you. The cooking tools are listed here, too, but you'll need to buy, beg, borrow or steal them from the store, your mother, ex-wife or girlfriend. We really don't have time to get involved in your personal domestic situation, except to encourage you to use the information in the book to try to improve that situation.

Your kitchen can be as creative and fun-filled as any office, workroom, ballpark or backseat you've ever occupied. With the proper tools and attitude, you will find it an environment full of potential for satisfaction in personal accomplishment.

Your kitchen requires certain equipment to help you cook. I've prepared a list of basic kitchen tools. I've also included some items that are not absolutely necessary, but are especially useful for specific tasks. You decide whether you want to obtain them now, or add them to your kitchen as your skills and interest increase.

By the way, gift-givers in your life now have a wide range of practical to ultra-progressive options to choose from for your birthday or holiday celebrations each year. There is an endless stream of time and energy-saving devices continually being invented to make your creative efforts in the kitchen easier and more fun.

LIFESAVER LIST

Mothers and sisters always seem to start from fully-equipped kitchens which spring from the formica counters like magic. Bachelors often need a little nudge to get out of the Mother Hubbard/Real Bare Cupboard Syndrome. So these are "must-steal" items for setting up your own chop shop.

A pot

A frying pan

A spatula (flipper)

Two knives (one sharp blade; one serrated blade so you can cut through soft dinner rolls without squishing them flat into pancakes)

A coffee cup

A glass

A knife, fork, spoon

A desire to acquire better implements before inviting guests over.

COOKING TOOLS

For those of you with steady work, begin to add these tools to your collection through purchase or by stopping in to see your aunt. Aunts always have five or six of each cooking item and would be happy to build you a care package of basic tools.

FOR COOKING

Casseroles	One, 2-quart (2 L); one, 3 (or 3½)-quart (3-3.5 L); and one, 5-6-quart (5-6 L). All with covers.
Double Boiler	1-quart (1 L). Each part can be used separately.
Frying pans	One pan 6-8" (15 -20 cm) in diameter and one 10-12" (25-30 cm) in diameter. Covers are optional here.
Large Kettle	8-10 quarts (8-10 L), with cover.
Loaf Pan	9" x 5" x 3" (2 L) size.
Roasting Pan	17" x 11" x 3" (5 L) size. May come with a roasting rack to fit, or may have roasting grooves in the bottom of the pan.
Saucepans	One each of 2-quart (2 L), 3 (or 3½)-quart (3 L) and 5-quart (5 L). All with lids.
Wok	Chinese frying pan (optional).

FOR MIXING

Consider these tools essential. They are used for every form of mixing . . . beating, whipping, creaming, stirring, blending, etc.

Hand blender   A sturdy construction and comfortable grip.

Metal spoons   Several convenient sizes.

Mixing bowls   A graduated set in stainless steel or glass.

Rotary beater   A sturdy, medium-size with a comfortable handle.

Rubber spatula   Standard size.

Wire wisk   8" or 10" (20 or 25 cm) size.

Wooden spoons   10" or 12" (25 or 30 cm) size, unvarnished wood.

FOR MEASURING

Correct measuring requires the proper tools. Always use level measurements of both liquid and dry ingredients . . . unless a recipe specifies otherwise.

Measuring spoons   A standard set of ¼ teaspoon (1 mL), ½ teaspoon (2 mL), 1 teaspoon (5 mL) and 1 tablespoon (15 mL).

Glass Measuring Cups   Use when measuring liquids; 1 cup (250 mL) size and ¼ cup (50 mL) size.

Metal Measuring Cups   Use for measuring dry ingredients; ¼ cup (50 mL), ⅓ cup (75 mL), ½ cup (125 mL) and 1 cup (250 mL).

Oven Thermometer   For gauging the degree of heat in an oven; use either column or dial type.

Meat Thermometer   For measuring the internal heat of meat; either round or column type. For the most accurate reading, insert the spiked end into the deepest part of the meat. Don't allow the spiked end to touch the bone or to rest in fat.

TEMPERATURE GUIDE

This guide should help you to make your way, successfully, through these recipes — and keep you from burning everything to a crisp.

Stove Top and Barbecue

Most stove top element controls are marked for high (very hot), medium (hot) and low (not so hot) heat. As you might surmise medium-low is somewhere in between medium and low. I'll leave you on your own for medium-high!

For barbecuing, or if your stove element controls are not marked, **hot** means that you can hold your hand about 3" (7 cm) above the heat source for 2-3 seconds, **medium** means that you can hold your hand there for about 4-6 seconds.

Oven

Very low oven	— 250-275 °F	= 120-140 °C
Low oven	— 275-325°F	= 140-160°C
Moderate oven	— 325-400°F	= 160-200°C
Hot oven	— 400-450°F	= 200-230°C
Very hot oven	— 450-550°F	= 230-285°C

FOR BAKING

Baking is a separate category of cooking and requires its own special equipment. The following equipment will cover the baking recipes in this cookbook.

Baking sheet   Either 8 x 10" (20 x 25 cm) or 10 x 12" (25 x 30 cm) size.

Pie pan   For recipes calling for a shallow casserole. 9" in diameter x 1" deep (1 L) size, either glass or metal.

Rectangular cake pan   13 x 9 x 2" (33 x 23 x 5 cm) size.

Rolling pin   A heavy 14" or 16" (35 or 40 cm) size.

Round cake pans   8" or 9" (20 or 23 cm) in diameter, 1½" (4 cm) deep.

Wire cooling racks   Slightly larger than the selected cake pan.

FOR CUTTING, CHOPPING, SLICING, DICING

Chopping board   16" x 20" (40 x 50 cm) in size and at least ¾" (2 cm) thick. Wooden chopping boards look great but they breed bacteria — try a new plastic chopping board.

Grater   A stand-up model with several sizes of teeth and a slicer.

Knives   10" (25 cm) bread knife with a serrated edge
10" (25 cm) cook's knife
10" (25 cm) ham or roast beef slicer
5" (13 cm) knife with a serrated edge
8" (20 cm) chopper
5" (13 cm) utility knife
A sharpening steel

AND FOR SPECIAL TASKS

Electric beater
Electric blender
Electric frying pan
Pasta maker

Electric can opener
Electric carving knife
Food processor

Some cooks consider these electric appliances as essential elements in their kitchen collection. You can buy them as a treat for yourself or as a gift for a fellow cook.

Those who wish to try the fondue dishes in this book will have to invest in (or borrow) a fondue pot.

COOKING TERMS

Bake	To cook in an oven by dry heat.
Baste	To keep food moist and add flavor while cooking, usually by spooning melted fat, pan juices, wine or other liquids over the surface of the food.
Beat	To mix ingredients together with a circular up and-down motion, using a whisk, a spoon or a rotary or electric beater.
Blanch	To plunge into boiling water to set the color and flavor of a vegetable, loosen the skin of a fruit or vegetable, remove excess salt, or precook.
Blend	To stir, rather than beat, ingredients until they are thoroughly combined.
Boil	To cook in a liquid whose temperature reaches 212°F (100°C), at sea level; the liquid surface is broken by a steady bubbling action.
Braise	To cook in a tightly covered pan with a small amount of liquid at a low temperature.
Brown	To turn the surface of food brown in color by cooking quickly in hot fat on top of the stove or at a high temperature in the oven.
Chill	To make cold, not frozen, in a refrigerator.
Chop	To cut into small pieces.
Coat	To cover entire surface of food with a given mixture.
Cool	To allow to stand until heat has reduced.
Cube	To cut into small, equal-size squares, usually ¼-½" (.6-1.3 cm).
Dash	A quick shake.
Dice	To cut into very small, even cubes.
Dot	To place small pieces of butter or other substances over the surface of food.
Drain	To remove liquid.
Dredge	To coat thoroughly with flour or other fine-grained ingredients.
Dust	To sprinkle lightly with flour or sugar.
Fry	To cook in hot fat. The oil in the pan reaches a depth of only ⅛" (.3 cm).
Garnish	To decorate or accompany a dish by adding other foodstuffs before serving.
Grease	To spread a film of fat on a surface (e.g. inside a pan).
Marinate	To allow vegetables and meat to stand seasoned in a liquid (with or without oil) to improve flavor and/or increase tenderness.
Parboil	To boil in a liquid until partially cooked.
Pare	To remove the peel and stem of a fruit or vegetable with a knife or other paring tool.
Pastry Bag	Also known as a "piping bag". Used with icing to decorate baked goods or with mashed potatoes to give a particular design to the surfaces of casseroles.

Preheat	To heat an oven or broiler to reach the desired temperature before using.
Purée	Any food blended to a liquid state.
Rolling Boil	A continuous regular boil with bubbles rolling toward the center of the saucepan from the edges.
Sauté	To cook food in a small amount of hot fat, over high heat, stirring and turning it frequently for even browning.
Season	To add salt, herbs, spices or other ingredients to increase the flavor of food.
Shred	To cut or shave food into thin pieces.
Simmer	To cook a liquid barely at the boiling point. The surface should show only a few bubbles breaking slowly.
Whip	To beat quickly and steadily, either by hand with a whisk or rotary beater or with an electric beater.

Bachelor's Guide Glossary

Catapult	To **chuck,** as in a medieval food fight, from one side of the room to another.
Chuck	Nickname for "Charles"; also, to **catapult** someone named Charles from one side of the room to another.
Fling	Young couple's activity in the spring; also, to **chuck** something considerably lighter than Charles in the general direction of the salad bowl.
Flip	Similar to **fling** except often involving the curled forefinger and thumb or entire body. Example: **Chuck catapulted** with joy when he heard the girl he had a **fling** with had *flipped* over him. (Of course, it's not always that simple!) The girl's boyfriend made a **flip** remark as he **flung** (past tense of **'fling'**) Chuck against the museum's only authentic **catapult.**
Heave	What Chuck did after being **flung** about; also to "toss up" as in "**Heave** the broccoli into the bowl, Harvey!"
Hurl	Similar to **heave** but usually with more emotion as in "She **hurled** my heavenly corned beef hash against the wall so I **heaved** her out into the street."
Improvise	To make up as you go along; what you do if you discover your refrigerator has been unplugged all day and the guests are due to arrive any minute. **Improvising** may include calling a caterer or having a pizza delivered.
Plop	What you do after a hard night of **improvising.**
Plunk	The sound something makes when it **plops** into place. These two terms are darn near interchangeable as food you **plunk** into place often makes a **plopping** sound as well.
Sling	Like **plunk** but done from a distance; also similar to **hurl**, but a **sling** is more of a side-arm **fling.**
Toss	To **fling** ingredients casually from a variety of angles and directions towards the same single target. To mix lightly until well-coated with a dressing (as in a salad!).

SPICES OF LIFE

Ever walk down that funny-smelling aisle in the grocery store on your way to picking up a new box of salt? The spice aisle: it's like Coney Island for the nose — almost odoriferous overkill.

Some of these spices are almost as old as food itself. Some began by being flavorful preservatives for different foods. Others have always brought out the flavors hidden within certain foods.

The following list includes spices mentioned in this book's recipes and a few others we thought you'd like to know about.

Basil: Used in green salads, vegetable soups, egg dishes, pastas and in many meat, fish and poultry dishes. Basil also works well with other herbs and can be used in vegetable dishes and Italian and other Mediterranean-style meals.

Chili Powder: Chili powder is a must in Chili Con Carne and Mexican and Spanish foods. It's also used in meat sauces, gravies, over roast potatoes, deviled eggs and cottage cheese. It can be added to tomato juice or cream-style corn to give a little taste "boost".

Cinnamon (ground): Cinnamon is used in fruit soups and sauces as well as spicy apples, pork chops, cottage cheese, cream cheese and French toast. It can also be sprinkled over custards, puddings, sweet potatoes, fruit salads or into eggnog. It is often used in pies, cinnamon buns or cinnamon toast. Sprinkle it over your regular toast, too!

Garlic Powder/Salt: When using garlic salt . . . use no other salt. Soups, gravies, casseroles, stews, meat sauces, fish, poultry and stuffings all benefit from the wise use of garlic salt. Other popular uses include: in vegetable soups or tomato-based BBQ sauces, over scrambled eggs or on garlic bread.

Nutmeg: Nutmeg is used in the crust of meat pies, in stews, fish casseroles, creamed chicken soup or on cauliflower, mashed potatoes and spinach. It is also used as a topping for eggnog, custards, doughnuts and other baked goods.

Onion Powder/Salt: Add this seasoning to cooked meats, soups, gravies, casseroles, stewed meats, fish, poultry, meat sauces, fish sauces, cheese sauces, stuffings or over scrambled eggs. It can be used in any recipe where a fresh onion is desired but unavailable. As with the garlic salt, when using onion salt, no other salt is necessary.

Oregano: Use oregano in meat sauces, gravies and beef stews. It also gives soups a lift. Rub some on lamb or pork before roasting. Potato salad, zucchini, eggplant and tomatoes also benefit from a bit of oregano.

Paprika: Paprika spices up chicken soup. Sprinkle some on fried pork chops, chicken, shellfish and fried fish or use it as a garnish for cheese and egg dishes.

Pepper (ground black): Use black pepper in soups, sauces, fish, meat and poultry dishes.

Pepper (ground white): Use white pepper anywhere in pale-colored sauces, soups, fish, meat, poultry and casseroles.

Rosemary: Used on roast chicken, lamb, pork, in spaghetti sauces, stuffing for poultry, over a mixed green salad, boiled potatoes and tomatoes.

Sage: Sage is wonderful with cream soups and chowders. Veal, goose, turkey, poultry and fish stuffings, seafood salads, roast pork and stuffed pork chops, meat loaf, hamburgers, casseroles, green salads, onions, tomatoes, Brussels sprouts, etc., etc., . . . (Get the picture?).

Seasoning Salt: Seasoning salt is good for many foods like eggs, vegetables, beef, lamb, pork, veal, poultry, baked fish, gravies and salads. BBQ meat and veggie flavors come alive with a little seasoning salt.

Thyme: (pronounced like "time") Thyme on your hands? Try putting it into soups, fish chowders, stuffings, sauces or over roast chicken or turkey. Thyme brightens up cottage cheese and pickled vegetables as well as Brussels sprouts and green peas.

APPENDIX C: FIFTY-THREE THRIFTY FREE TIPS

FOR EFFECTIVE SHOPPING:

1. Always shop with a list of specific items to purchase.
2. Check the "Best Before. . ." date on products. Take particular care to ensure freshness with milk, yogurt and cheeses. Pick from the second or third row deep in the cooler as often those foods which expire earliest will be placed at the front.
3. Pick only the best-looking foods and leave those with any mold, discoloration, or strange smell. Let the grocery store staff know how you feel about less than satisfactory food on the shelves.
4. Read the labels to check for enrichment and ingredients.
5. Leave damaged cans, open packages or dirty products on the store shelf.
6. Buy fresh fruit and vegetables when they are in season.
7. For the best flavors and textures, perishables like meat, fruit and vegetables should be bought at the last possible moment.
8. Watch for sales and use coupons.
9. Get to know a good butcher. Ask for advice from grocery store staff.
10. Store brands are usually more economical than nationally advertised brands.
11. Remember low-cost foods are just as nutritious as expensive foods.
12. If you don't have proper storage facilities for leftovers, buy in the exact quantities you require for each meal.
13. If you do have proper storage or freezer facilities, buy in large amounts (of meat, for example) and freeze portions for future meals. That way you take advantage of specials on certain kinds of foods.
14. If you have a freezer, buy bread on special and freeze it. It will keep for two months.
15. Check groceries on shelves above and below eye level. You will often find good buys.
16. When you buy frozen fish, ask the butcher to saw the fish into suitable serving slices.
17. Never shop when hungry.

FOR EFFECTIVE MEAL PLANNING:

18. Make a list of all the foods you need before you shop. It can be very frustrating (and a waste of time) to begin to prepare a meal without all the ingredients. Do you improvise, substitute, change plans, or dash back to the store?
19. Looking ahead for a week and planning all three meals each day guarantees effective shopping, a balanced diet and the best use of leftovers.
20. Read newspaper columns on food to gather new ideas and remain aware of food bargains.
21. It helps to remember what season it is. Are all the foods you require for your meal available? Are more reasonably priced "in season" foods just as suitable?
22. Check and clean cutlery and glassware. Spots, smudges, dust or cracks on plates and utensils do not set the appropriate tone for the evening.
23. Prepare foods only in the amounts needed for the upcoming meal.

FOR EFFECTIVE MEAL PREPARATION:

24. Have a plan for the use of utensils, stove burners and the oven, and also for the preparation and serving dishes to prevent unpleasant surprises.
25. Write down preparation times so that all dishes are ready for serving when you want to serve them.
26. Think about the oven and refrigerator space necessary.
27. Read your recipes and list everything you're going to need — even salt and pepper. This can help prepare your grocery list and prevent those last minute dashes to the convenience store.
28. Can anything be made and frozen in advance? Allow enough time for marinades and heating or cooling periods before and during the meal.
29. Prepare raw fruits and vegetables immediately prior to serving or keep them in the refrigerator until serving.
30. Cook vegetables in skins whenever possible for maximum nutrient retention . . . keep those vegetable vitamin goodies going in the right direction.
31. Cooking for one or two is much easier with properly sized equipment. Small or individual casserole or loaf pans make more sense for singles.

FOR EFFECTIVE HANDLING OF FOOD:

32. Bacteria are everywhere — in the house, on raw foods, on counter tops, on your hands and in your hair. Keep food preparation tables and counters clean. Avoid placing dirty dishes, bottles, or cartons on them when you are preparing food. You only have to get sick once with food poisoning to understand why we harp on this.
33. Any cuts, sores, burns, or boils should be covered with waterproof bandages while preparing food. Such infections can harbor food poisoning bacteria.
34. Thoroughly wash utensils, fresh fruit, vegetables and the preparation area before beginning to use them.
35. Use a clean utensil to taste food during preparation.
36. All raw and cooked meat should be refrigerated unless the package states that the product can be kept at room temperature. The same principle is true for cooked veggies, milk and milk products and dressings.
37. When in doubt about moldy foods, such as cheese or jam, play it safe and throw them away. When in doubt — toss it out!
38. Never partially cook poultry the day before final cooking. If you start, make sure to finish the job; then refrigerate until required.
39. Never store cleaning or disinfecting agents, pesticides and other poisonous substances in food areas.
40. To avoid cross contamination, carry raw and cooked meats to and from the barbecue on separate platters. Wash knives after using them on one food and before using them on another.

FOR EFFECTIVE MEAL PRESENTATION:

41. Serve hot food on hot plates and cold food on cold plates.
42. Food should be arranged neatly on plates or platters.
43. A garnish such as a sprig of parsley, a twist of lemon, or bright red tomato slices brighten up the main course presentation.
44. Foods of clashing colors such as bright red tomatoes and purple beets should not be served together.
45. Choose interesting plate shapes or different kinds of pottery to use as serving dishes.
46. Cloth napkins and napkin rings dress up a table quite nicely and they really impress a special date.
47. If you place candles on or against a mirrored surface, the reflection doubles the pleasing effect.

FOR EFFECTIVE FOOD STORAGE (LEFTOVERS INCLUDED):

48. Store canned goods at room temperature.
49. Wrap foods for the freezer carefully in air-tight packaging for maximum vitamin retention.
50. The "best before" date on many dairy products, eggs and packaged meats means that food will be at its best, if properly stored, up to that date. The foods may still be edible after that date but may have changed in quality or nutritive value.
51. Remove stuffing from cooked meat, fish or poultry before cooling and storing. Refrigerate stuffing in a separate container.
52. Some people find an emergency shelf or cupboard helpful to cover those surprise visits from friends or to help out on those days when the weather prevents you from shopping. A variety of canned fruits and vegetables, peanut butter, and frozen meat pies can make quick, handy meals.
53. These thrifty tips have been generously shared with us from a range of public service pamphlets and brochures. Contact your local board of health, library, natural gas or utilities company, regional or national agricultural marketing boards and gather your own free collection of helpful hints.

INDEX

167

THE BACHELOR'S GUIDE TEAM

Clarence Shields, Project Coordinator

Upon completing university in the early 70's, Clarence joined his family's business in the operation of an A & W in Fort McMurray, Alberta.

This A & W was the first in Canada to earn over $1 million in gross sales and repeated this achievement three years in a row.

Clarence coordinated the planning, construction, and operation of six restaurants and administered a staff of over 300.

Always a fan of good cooking, Clarence has contributed to the industry in Alberta as a founding member of the Fort McMurray Academy of Chefs de Cuisine. He spearheaded the first apprenticeship cooking program in Fort McMurray with Keyano College, and co-developed the first Alberta Food and Beverage Service Training Program. He is former Vice-President of the Alberta Restaurant Association, responsible for Industry Education.

Clarence's promotional and marketing skills have been recognized by the Canadian Food Service Industry. He was awarded the Best Promotion of the Month in North America in the food service and hospitality industry by Cameron's Food Service Promotions Reporter.

Clarence's skills in human resource development enable him to excite and motivate people and reinforce individual accomplishments in the art of good cooking.

Darrin Ames, Chef

Darrin was born and educated in Red Deer, Alberta. He completed his apprenticeship as a chef in Fort McMurray after a three-year training program at the Northern Alberta Institute of Technology.

At the age of 19 he was inducted into the Canadian Federation of Chefs de Cuisine as their youngest member ever. His ultimate goals include, of course, owning his own restaurant and becoming a member of Team Canada's Cooks when the competitions are held at the Olympics.

As an Interprovincial Red Seal Chef, Darrin's professional qualifications are recognized nationwide. He was a part of the team preparing and presenting the wedding feast for Wayne Gretzky and Janet Jones in July 1988.

His work experience as an Executive Chef covers a wide range of food and beverage management responsibilities, from large banquet facilities, fast food and family restaurants to more upscale dining establishments.

His training in management and food and labor cost analysis contribute to his concern for the pocketbook of the new-to-the-kitchen cook.

THE BACHELOR'S GUIDE TEAM

Yardley Jones, Illustrator

Yardley was born at a very early age in Liverpool, England, raised in a sparsely populated Welsh mining town and received an education to match.

After studying architecture and majoring in poaching, mountain climbing and boxing, he now keeps fit by running in marathons all over the world.

Yardley's cartoons have been published in most major daily and weekly publications in the U.K., including the prestigious PUNCH magazine.

In 1957, he and his newly acquired bride immigrated to Canada. He has been the editorial cartoonist on THE EDMONTON JOURNAL(5 years), THE TORONTO TELEGRAM (6 years), THE MONTREAL STAR (8 years) and THE EDMONTON JOURNAL (4 years). Currently with THE EDMONTON JOURNAL as "roving cartoonist" working in color, Yardley's work has been syndicated in most major U.S. and Canadian daily newspapers as well as TIME and NEWSWEEK magazines.

The original artwork from many of his cartoons has been hung in the offices of every Canadian Prime Minister and President of the U.S.A. since 1968. Another original, requested by the Royal Family, hangs in Buckingham Palace.

Six books of his collected works have been published and his work has appeared on national television. CARTOONING WITH YARDLEY JONES is a 26-episode TV series teaching the fundamentals of cartooning with the emphasis on FUN! His accompanying guidebook has helped hundreds of new cartoonists sharpen their skills and develop their own personal styles.

Fred Keating, Writer

Fred is best known to Canadians as the producer/host of 161 episodes of MAILBAG and the host of MOVIEWEEK. These programs were broadcast on First Choice/Superchannel and over 400 cable affiliates nationwide from 1982-86. Recent surveys reveal one out of ten Canadians are familiar with Keating's sorting out of film and video issues. His television "Special Reports" include programs on such diverse topics as hazardous waste, severe storms, financial planning, and development in the far north.

In addition to writing and hosting several television series on the ACCESS Network, producing and hosting a province-wide performing arts radio show, CENTRE STAGE, for 6 years, and appearing in six feature films, Fred's writing credits for entertaining print or video teaching materials include clients such as the Calgary 1988 Winter Olympics, Shell Canada, Petro-Canada, Dow Canada, Syncrude, and Marlin Travel. He hosted the Miss Grey Cup Pageant 1984, wrote and hosted the live television broadcast of the Alberta Film and Television Awards for years, and continues to host CBC's annual production of the Lion's Christmas Telethon.

Fred claims he only took down notes as relayed to him by the reclusive Clarence "Culinary" Culpepper and other members of the Culpepper Clan.

Share *The Bachelor's Guide* with a friend

Order *The Bachelor's Guide* at $15.95 per book plus $2.00 (total order) for shipping and handling.

Number of books _____ x 15.95 = $ _____

Postage and handling _____ = $ _____2.00

Subtotal _____ = $ _____

In Canada add 7% GST _____(Subtotal x .07) = $ _____

Total enclosed _____ = $ _____

U.S. and international orders payable in U.S. funds./ Price is subject to change.

NAME: _____

STREET: _____

CITY: _____ PROV./STATE _____

COUNTRY _____ POSTAL CODE/ZIP _____

Please make cheque or money order payable to: **Normac Publishing Ltd.**
4104 - 149 Street
Edmonton, Alberta
Canada   T6H 5L9

For fund raising or volume purchases, contact **Normac Publishing Ltd.** for volume rates.

Please allow 3-4 weeks for delivery

Share *The Bachelor's Guide* with a friend

Order *The Bachelor's Guide* at $15.95 per book plus $2.00 (total order) for shipping and handling.

Number of books _____ x 15.95 = $ _____

Postage and handling _____ = $ _____2.00

Subtotal _____ = $ _____

In Canada add 7% GST _____(Subtotal x .07) = $ _____

Total enclosed _____ = $ _____

U.S. and international orders payable in U.S. funds./ Price is subject to change.

NAME: _____

STREET: _____

CITY: _____ PROV./STATE _____

COUNTRY _____ POSTAL CODE/ZIP _____

Please make cheque or money order payable to: **Normac Publishing Ltd.**
4104 - 149 Street
Edmonton, Alberta
Canada   T6H 5L9

For fund raising or volume purchases, contact **Normac Publishing Ltd.** for volume rates.

Please allow 3-4 weeks for delivery